BWB Texts

Short books on big subjects
for Aotearoa New Zealand

The Economic Possibilities of Decolonisation

MATTHEW SCOBIE
AND ANNA STURMAN

Contents

Introduction

This is a book about capitalism and decolonisation; the two are intrinsically linked, and understanding that link is essential for taking Aotearoa forward. We are in a long historical arc that is being bent towards decolonisation.[1] To continue to bend this arc in the future, we have to know how we got here. To know how we got here and where we might go, we need to take Māori economic perspectives seriously. The future of Aotearoa depends on how Māori engage with capitalism.[2]

We are writing this book in partnership as a Kāi Tahu and a Pākehā scholar. We do so with Te Tiriti o Waitangi as a metaphor, putting forward ideas from a rangatiratanga perspective and a kāwanatanga perspective which, together, become our relational perspective. This metaphor for writing is inspired by the 'spheres of influence' framework developed by *Matike Mai*, the independent working group on constitutional transformation, which articulates three areas of governance: the kāwanatanga sphere (the Crown's influence), rangatiratanga sphere (Māori influence) and a relational sphere (working together).[3] It has become very clear that Te Tiriti creates a basis for dual legal systems; we argue that, by the same token, there are or could be *at least* dual economic systems. In this book we explore those systems – Māori economies and colonial-capitalism – and the boundaries between the two where road maps for the future may emerge. This brings us to our central question: what are the economic realities and possibilities of decolonisation in Aotearoa?

By decolonisation we mean dismantling unjust colonial structures, reimagining and reconstructing Indigenous lifeways (ways of meeting physical, spiritual and social needs), and establishing just relationships among peoples of Aotearoa into the future. Any discussion of colonialism in Aotearoa that tiptoes around capitalism is incomplete. But any discussion of capitalism that tiptoes around colonialism is also incomplete. Both must be explored together to understand the challenges we face. Following others, we use the term colonial-capitalism to describe this relationship.[4]

The story we tell in this book is broadly as follows: Māori economies were and are distinct from what we know as 'the economy' now. Prior to European contact and colonisation, Māori economies were on their own paths, with perspectives and practices that could have developed in different ways. Not all economies are on a single, inevitable path towards capitalism. Capitalism emerged in particular conditions in Britain, and as it pushed against the limits of that context, a 'fix' was required for it to keep expanding.[5] Colonial-capitalism was that fix.

As capitalists and workers as well as missionaries and a range of other people emigrated from Britain, Māori welcomed many of these newcomers, much of their technology and some of the opportunities they brought. This typically occurred on Māori terms. Prior to systematic colonisation, Māori were engaging with aspects of the encroaching capitalist economy as an opportunity to advance wellbeing, and in many cases doing so within their existing economic perspectives. But this wasn't enough of a fix for an ailing British capitalism, which required new resources (land and labour) and more profitable activities to invest in if it was to continue expanding. Absolute private property and a social system to regulate it were needed. This in turn required the severance of tangata (people) from whenua (place): that is, the severance of Māori from their lands. However, land wasn't private property for Māori. Whenua was a relation – the placenta of Papatūānuku, who tangata were, and are, also descended from. As part of the fix for British capitalism, tangata had to be severed from whenua in Aotearoa so that whenua could be transformed into private property. Absolute private property is central to capitalism.

The settler government was disproportionately funded by dispossessed Māori whenua, which was on-sold to provide capital for the emerging settler economy. Dispossessed tangata were later forced to provide labour for this same economy to meet the basic necessities of life. This new economy, gradually at times and rapidly at others, encroached on Māori so that what were once opportunities to engage with new economies and technologies were now imperatives to survive. What started as the Crown's extra-economic powers (legal, political, or military superiority and coercion) gradually laid the foundations for economic powers (where survival depends on obeying market forces). These extra-economic powers, starting with Te Tiriti and then breaches of Te Tiriti, established the economic power that continued dispossession through indirect means.[6]

However, this process was never complete or total. Māori have always and will always resist and provide space for alternatives. This resistance may be within, at the edges of or beyond colonial-capitalism. These spaces of resistance provide some hope for possible economic futures that are socially and environmentally just. The answer to our question – what are the economic realities and possibilities of decolonisation? – is that there are a multitude of possibilities, though they are constrained by contemporary realities. We have to work through the constraints to enact the possibilities. This brings to the fore our fundamental argument that Māori economies both stabilise colonial-capitalism and prefigure alternative possibilities – a 'stabilisation–prefiguration dynamic'.

With this broad argument in mind, we have structured the book as follows:

In Chapter One, we set out the theoretical and academic foundations of our argument. This section is quite dense and complex, but please bear with us. Our complex realities require nuanced theories.

In Chapter Two, we introduce the importance of understanding Māori economic organisation prior to colonisation. This is reasonably well documented but not generally considered essential for economic theory, policy and practice.[7] We believe that within these forms of economic organisation there are possibilities for the future. We focus on several key features that act as a framework throughout the book: obligations, rights and resources; exchange and distribution; and labour.

In Chapter Three we start at the point of Māori contact with Europeans and explore three primary periods of this time that illuminate our economic reality: contact through to Te Tiriti; dispossession; and Treaty settlements. The early period can shed light on what things looked like when Māori had the opportunity to engage with the encroaching economy to some extent on their own terms. The second period illustrates the fundamental role that dispossession played in replacing Māori economies with colonial-capitalism through changed property relations. The most recent period explores the opportunities and challenges that modern Treaty settlements present. These summaries contribute to our understanding of dual economies under Te Tiriti.

Chapter Four explores diverse economic practices in Aotearoa today. These suggest that aspects of the Māori economy have persevered despite repression by colonial-capitalism. This forms a key part of our overall argument that Māori economic perspectives can inform the future of Aotearoa's political economy. We support this by exploring the links and contradictions between a post-settlement organisation – Te Rūnanga Group, and its economic practices – and the diverse and layered economic practices of whānau and hapū that coalesce into the iwi of Ngāi Tahu. These are not synonymous but interdependent. In doing so, we distinguish between Māori businesses in the colonial-capitalist economy, and Māori economies made up of Māori institutions, to reveal some of the challenges and opportunities of the contemporary context. We focus on Ngāi Tahu for two main reasons. First, Matthew is Ngāi Tahu (although he started from a place of intergenerational disconnection) and has done the majority of his research with the iwi. Second, Ngāi Tahu were early to 'settle' in the modern Treaty settlements framework, and this gives us some distance to explore what has happened since, and where to next.

Chapter Five concludes the book by asking a set of further questions. We offer some tentative answers, but suggest that these questions are most appropriately answered with or by communities working together. Our main argument here is that Māori economies do provide some possibilities for addressing Aotearoa's pressing problems, but these possibilities need to be explored in the context of constraining realities. We make three related points in summary. First, there is a 'stabilisation versus prefiguration' dynamic at the boundary between colonial-capitalism and Māori economies. By this we mean that Māori economies can stabilise capitalism by providing care for people and places that capitalism needs but does not value, but this care for people and place can be used to prefigure (that is, imagine and demonstrate the possibility of) alternative futures. Second, there can be no economic transformation without constitutional transformation, and a just constitutional transformation requires economic transformation. Third, Māori economic perspectives can help inform future economies.

We rely heavily on the thoughts and scholarship of those who have come before us, and have done our best to be transparent about where our ideas emerge from. There is a large body of scholarship from across the globe that has heavily influenced our thinking. This includes but is not limited to the work of: Tā Tipene O'Regan, Te Maire Tau, Michael Stevens, Angela Wanhalla, Maria Bargh, Ani Mikaere, Margaret Mutu, Moana Jackson, Simon Barber, Emmy Rakete, Morgan Godfery, Paul Tapsell, Mānuka Hēnare, Atholl Anderson, John Reid, Catherine Comyn, Matt Wynyard, Evan Poata-Smith, Danielle Webb, Glen Sean Coulthard, Leanne Betasamosake Simpson, Nick Estes, Audra Simpson, Art Manuel, Ellen Meiksins Wood, E.P. Thompson, Raymond Firth, Hazel Petrie, Brian Easton, Jane Kelsey, Karl Marx, Onur Ulas Ince, James O'Connor, Neil Smith, Natasha Heenan, Matthew Ryan, Stuart Rosewarne, Danielle Celermajer, Ariel Salleh, Mary Mellor, Matt Rout, Keith Hooper, Kate Kearins, Martin Fisher and Lise Vogel. We owe a great debt to all of these and others, and hope that our contribution to the conversation is constructive. At the same time, we take full responsibility for our writing and interpretations of existing work.

1. Theoretical Framework

An Historical Materialist Approach

Different theoretical traditions have examined the emergence and ongoing operation of capitalism.[1] In the following we set out a very condensed version of an historical materialist approach.[2] This historical materialist approach challenges the grand assumptions of neoclassical economics by suggesting that the 'economic' does not float untethered above the world, guided by universal and ahistorical human characteristics such as the 'rational economic man'.[3] Rather, what we call the economy is one aspect of a mode of production: that is, 'the social activity and the social relations through which human beings interact with nature in producing the conditions of life', the social, cultural and political aspects of which evolve over time.[4] Today, in Aotearoa, we live in a locally mediated capitalist mode of production within a global capitalist economy, the determining force of which is profit.[5] This means that, while other forms of production exist at different scales, like subsistence economies, cooperatives, commons and, indeed, Māori economies, the dominant system of organising the production and exchange of the resources we all need to live is structured by the imperatives of capitalism. Prior to systematic dismantling, Māori economies were a mode of production in which profit was not the determining force.

An historical materialist approach begins with familiar concepts (the economy, the state and politics) but is concerned with revealing their internal structures and enabling transformation towards a better world.[6] The Political Marxist tradition within an historical materialist approach is particularly concerned with reminding us that all social relations are underpinned by power, are not inevitable and can be changed. This means paying attention to how historically specific forms of social organisation (how we make our day-to-day decisions, such as what to eat or where to live) emerge and are stabilised or destabilised.

The beginnings of capitalism (the 'what')

Capitalism emerged in Britain in the sixteenth century. The exact time and specifics have long been argued, but there is little doubt about what made this form of social organisation unique and world-changing.[7] One factor was the capital relation.[8] Others were new relationships to the environment determined by the capital relation; new forms of political power and responsibility; and an internal imperative for expansion.

The capital relation was central to the emerging mode of production, with wage-labour or labour as a commodity. This created the definitive labour–capital opposition. The capital relation required the destruction of previously existing social relationships and the establishment of a group of people who had nothing but their labour, transformed into a commodity, as a means to access the basic necessities of life. This process has been referred to as primitive accumulation. The initial wave of primitive accumulation created the first 'working class' who were cut loose from their lifeways. In this perspective, class is a relationship to the means of production (the physical and abstract resources used to produce goods and services as commodities), rather than an objective location within a hierarchy. Capitalists create profits by selling commodities for more than it costs to produce them, including the wages of workers. Capitalists increase profits by forcing down costs of production through the depression of wages and increasing the intensity of labour through increased mechanisation (known as increasing the organic composition of capital). This requires capitalists to appropriate (claim) the surplus value created by workers. Workers are thus alienated from the commodities and surplus value that they have been a part of creating, and become instruments of production. This is one form of alienation in historical materialism, and is often referred to as exploitation.

Wage-labour is central to reproducing the working class in capitalism. A great deal of 'free' human labour and natural resources are also relied on, in large part to lower the wages the capitalist must pay the worker. 'Social reproduction' and variations refer to the unwaged or undervalued and often unrecognised labour of reproducing ourselves, our families and communities, and the environments that sustain us in capitalism.[9] These relations are required for the 'formal economy' of wage-labour to tick along, producing and distributing commodities, but are typically not recognised and valued. The work of social reproduction within capitalism is also uneven across gender and race.[10] The so-called 'incompleteness' of capitalism in part refers to this immense amount of social reproduction, which is appropriated yet not formally supported by the capitalist economy.[11] We bring social reproduction into our discussion to illustrate how these necessary but invisible forms of labour – for example, Māori and gendered labour – might be made visible and incorporated in alternative futures. We will use the terms reproduction and reproducing, appropriation and appropriated in this way throughout the book.

We also use alienation in another sense. Human relationships with the rest of nature were altered in line with this new form of social organisation. Karl Marx described this change as a 'metabolic rift'. Humans were alienated from established rhythms of reproducing themselves, their families and communities, and people migrated towards places where wage-labour was available. This is another side of alienation in historical materialism: humans become alienated from existing connections to nature, and from what it means to be human. This severance caused a deep rift between urban and rural spaces in early capitalism. As demand and consumption concentrated in urban spaces, production of raw materials in the rural spaces systematically stripped soils of nutrients, and overwhelmed urban spaces to which these materials were transported with waste.[12] By severing alternative lifeways to ensure that people had to labour for wages just to live, capitalism set in motion exploitation as the engine of economic growth but revealed itself as fundamentally unsustainable.[13]

As part of the development of these new social relations, old feudal forms of power were gradually transformed.[14] Though these feudal forms involved parasitic property relations between lord and serf, they also involved complex social obligations, and these were transformed by the emerging forms of private property and political power that coalesced in the capitalist state.[15] A veneer of equality was established, while deep material inequalities with reduced social obligations were obscured. An example of this veneer of equality is the gradual extension of the franchise beyond white propertied males, culminating in 'one person, one vote'.

We must also distinguish between commerce and capitalism. Many types of non-capitalist commerce have existed and do exist, wherein various classes of people own the means of production or subsistence and have opportunities to trade. The simple logic of trade is an exchange of reciprocal requirements; it does not necessarily generate the need to maximise profit and to produce competitively. In some of these non-capitalist systems, dominant classes and rulers rely on 'extra-economic' powers of appropriation for their commercial advantage. What distinguishes capitalism from these are the particular social relations that generate market imperatives to maximise profit and to produce competitively.[16] The power of profit to determine social obligations and norms is a dynamic that brings capitalism into conflict with alternative economies that may precede it or persevere at its peripheries.

Finally, the requirement for growth that is hard-wired into capitalism means that it is inherently expansionary.[17]

Part of the fundamental opposition between labour and capital derives from the drive to lower the costs of production, meaning labour, to maximise profits and invest in innovation to keep ahead of competition. Competition in capitalism also drives the dynamic of externalisation, or the shifting of costs to third parties. It does so by forcing capitalists to lower costs, including costs of labour and protecting the environment, to remain competitive. These pressures mean that no permanent compromise to stabilise the system is possible, and crises persist.[18] As David Harvey writes:

> Capitalism is highly dynamic and inevitably expansionary. Powered by the engine of accumulation for accumulation's sake and fuelled by the exploitation of labour power, it constitutes a permanently revolutionary force which perpetually reshapes the world we live in.[19]

Colonialism and the necessary expansion of capitalism (the 'how')

In *The Financial Colonisation of Aotearoa,* Catherine Comyn lays out the relationship between capitalism in Britain and colonialism in Aotearoa.[20] Like Comyn, we believe that awareness of the messy birth of capitalism in Britain is important both for understanding the 'costs' of introducing the system and for unveiling the 'costs' of its ongoing operation.[21] These costs were and are not purely financial but include the social, environmental, cultural and other burdens unevenly borne by the people and places implicated in the transformations.

Colonialism is an ongoing process of domination and extraction, binding and altering pre-existing lifeways in service to an expanding system of power. Though colonialism long predates capitalism, colonialism has proven necessary to capitalism. Indeed, we can point to the imperative of capitalism (the drive to expand in order to stall crisis) as a central driver of systematic colonisation in Aotearoa. The initial attempts to extend the power of the British Crown over Aotearoa and to erase Māori sovereignty were the seeds of the future capitalist state. We contrast this imposition of sovereignty with contact, where there was no attempted extension of systematic colonisation over the encountered. We also make a distinction between systematic colonisation and contact to make the point that systematic colonisation was not inevitable. Māori could have had access to the technologies and lifeways introduced through contact without the systematic colonisation that followed.

A key concept for understanding the relationship between colonialism and capitalism is primitive accumulation. Many Indigenous and Māori thinkers have returned to primitive accumulation in the context of decolonisation.[22] This concept challenges Adam Smith, who suggested that capitalism emerged because some people work hard and accumulate more, while some people are lazy and prefer to work for the hard workers. Marx, on the other hand, made it clear that things like slavery, colonialism, commons enclosure, predatory lending and violence were fundamental to the origins of capitalism. He analysed the historical experience of divorcing people from their means of production to lay these origins bare. Many people did not enthusiastically engage in wage-labour as long as they had alternatives, so, under capitalism, these alternatives had to be destroyed.[23] Marx actually used Edward Gibbon Wakefield's plans for 'systematic colonisation' of Aotearoa (discussed further in Chapter Three) to demonstrate his argument that capitalism violently expropriates in order to exist.[24]

Writing in the early twentieth century, Rosa Luxemburg updated Marx's argument to suggest that primitive accumulation was not just the beginning of capitalism, but was required for its continued existence. Capitalism always needs scope to continue expanding, responding to the growth imperative which drives the system as a whole. Luxemburg called this imperialism, and while there are other strands of thinking around imperialism, we stick with the one that sees it as a state-enabled fix to capitalist expansion. By this we mean using the powers of the state to bring new land and labour into markets, and defer crises of under- or over-production in the existing capitalist system.[25]

Yellowknives Dene First Nations scholar Glen Coulthard argues that just because non-Indigenous critical theorists have ranged from condescending to outright racist, it does not mean that Indigenous peoples should abandon non-Indigenous critical theory. He brought primitive accumulation front and centre into Indigenous thinking and resistance by arguing that it is an ongoing process but need not be violent. It is a feature of the liberal politics of settler colonies that require Indigenous lands and lifeways to remain open for capitalist development. Simon Barber argues that the key transition for Ngāi Tahu specifically, but also Māori more broadly, was the forced transition from tangata whenua to labour and property.[26] We take up this discussion in Chapter Three.

Luxemburg and Coulthard explore capitalism's relationship to its outside: external frontiers expanding outwards, accumulating new spaces and peoples. Authors like Silvia Federici highlight internal frontiers such as the control of women's bodies. These external and internal frontiers of expansion provide the link between primitive accumulation and social reproduction, both of which acknowledge time and space within, at the edges of and beyond capitalism. This incompleteness of capitalism does not prevent the existence of alternatives, but these alternatives present frontiers for accumulation and so are always in danger of being transformed into commodities.[27] Capitalism is unable to exist by itself, but can also tolerate no rival at its side.[28] However, the 'free' labour associated with social reproduction, required to prevent the degradation of people and the rest of nature past the point of use to capital, is necessary to the functioning of capitalism.

So in contrast to representations of capitalism as forming naturally and inevitably, the social organisation of capitalism took, and continues to take, massive extra-economic power to construct and to force upon people.[29] Key to the assertion of capitalist social relations, including property relations, is the attempted destruction of all other social forms, and this happens most effectively through the removal of alternative lifeways. For Indigenous peoples, with lifeways that are opposed to the individualism and externalisation required in capitalist systems, settler colonial assertions of sovereignty are devastating.[30] This is one of the great tragedies of capitalism's ongoing expansion: people who were forcibly dispossessed of the means of subsistence and alternative lifeways in the transition to capitalism in Britain would go on to enact these processes across the world. Their descendants continue to do so today. This system is now global, and engaging with it is imperative for survival.

Colonial-capitalism (the global web of life)

> As an analytic framework, colonial capitalism rests on the fundamental premise that capitalism has historically emerged within the juridico-political framework of the 'colonial empire' rather than the 'nation-state'. It grasps capitalist relations as having developed in and through colonial networks of commodities, peoples, ideas, and practices, which formed a planetary web of value chains connecting multiple and heterogeneous sites of production across oceanic distances.[31]

For us, this point made by Onur Ulas Ince means that through colonialism, Aotearoa was being drawn into not only the British Empire but also the development of global capitalism. Colonialism occurred in this case because of the requirement for resources – land and labour – to mitigate the tendency for the rate of profit to fall. This tendency occurs as a result of the competition between capitalists to sell their commodities – products and services – for profit. Profits tend to equalise over time as innovations in technologies and processes become industry standards.[32] For example, the first firm to use a new method of production would be able to generate supernormal profits until other firms adopted that same method of production, reducing the competitive advantage of that first mover. Firms must innovate new advantages, or cut costs (e.g. inputs like land and labour) to remain viable. Further, the destruction of established ways of life in the protracted, violent transformation to capitalism in Britain created a working class who were increasingly fractious about the process. Encouraging (or dispatching) these people to colonise fresh land on the other side of the world was one method of minimising the threat of outright revolution in the birthplace of capitalism.[33]

Edward Gibbon Wakefield, who was a key player in the New Zealand Company, was so deeply concerned about the state of capitalism in Britain that he authored a book of letters called *A View of The Art of Colonization.*[34] 'Colonization,' he claimed, 'is a natural means of seeking relief from the worst of our social ills, and of thus averting formidable political dangers.'[35] For him, these social ills derived from a superabundance of capital, that led to excessive competition and a penchant for reckless gambling, resulting in crisis and ruin. The primary political danger was worker-led revolution, the spectre of which haunted Europe: 'Thus far, the education of the common people has not improved their lot; it has only made them discontented with it,' he wrote. 'The present fruits of popular education in this country are Chartism and socialism.'[36]

So rather than redistributing that superabundant capital to give workers better lives and improve their lot, his fix was systematic colonisation.[37] 'The object they had in view was, in general terms, to substitute systematic colonization for mere emigration, and on a scale sufficient to produce important effects on the mother-country.'[38] It would not be enough to merely send people over to the colonies; the institutions of the mother country (the capitalist state) were required so that the capitalist class system could be extended out as well. Wakefield used the term 'colonial capitalist' to describe the sort of people who needed to populate the colonies to keep the system going.

The emphasis on colonial-capitalism as global in nature is important. It ties the local experiences of colonisation to a profoundly earth-altering system of extraction and distribution according to profit imperatives, rather than to any other system of production and exchange. Those alternative social relations, however, are never able to be completely destroyed, because capitalism relies on non-capitalist human and non-human lifeways to exist. This push and pull is a constitutive dynamic of capitalism; it severs communities from alternative means of subsistence to force them into wage-labour, yet demands that these networks of care and regeneration persist, to lower costs for capital.

Lifeways at the edge of capitalism are therefore of utmost importance in assessing opportunities to restore relationships between people and the environment that prioritise the needs of people and place before profits. It is our broad contention that an expanded understanding of Māori economies and how they survive within and against the dominance of capitalism can help us to address the social, ecological and economic crises we currently face. The connection between Indigenous peoples and sovereignty, and the working classes of colonising populations, is an important part of this discussion. In sum, we argue that Māori can and will be agents of economic transformation in Aotearoa; decolonisation therefore both requires and is required for it.

2. Economies of Mana

Pre-colonial Māori Economies

We must know where we have come from in order to navigate the future successfully. For Aotearoa this means knowing how the economy was organised by Māori prior to and in the early years of European contact and colonisation. This chapter provides a brief exploration of key features in Māori economies: obligations, rights and resources; exchange and distribution; and labour. We take care to use Māori 'economies' because there was no single fixed way of doing things; different groups engaged in diverse economic practices to achieve their livelihoods.[1] They still do. We use economies in an expansive sense to mean how societies reproduce themselves in and through the rest of nature. Critical to Māori economies, though, is the concept of mana (authority). The centrality of mana has resulted in the framing 'economy or economies of mana', generally associated with the late Dr Mānuka Hēnare.[2]

Māori economies are not 'pre-capitalist' in the sense that they were just sitting there waiting to evolve on an inevitable path into capitalism. They were and are something different. Using contemporary concepts to understand what occurred in the past can be problematic – we need historically specific tools to understand historically specific phenomena. We carry on carefully, highlighting these difficulties where possible.

A key starting point is that culture, land, plants, water, animals and economy were all intimately related to one another.[3] Culture was not something that floated untethered above politics and economics, as it is sometimes framed today, but was woven throughout. Culture was a mode of production or, more appropriately, a mode of life.[4] Culture influenced economic, social and environmental relations, and vice versa.[5] It was not necessarily about controlling the means of production to extract profit, but about stewarding the means of reproduction.[6] By reproduction, again we mean the ability for Māori to meet physical, spiritual and social needs – an expansive idea of reproduction that we refer to as 'lifeways'. This history speaks to the present day, because not only is controlling production out of the hands of most people, especially Māori, but sites of reproduction like housing, health, and child and elder care are becoming increasingly unattainable through waves of commodification; that is, homes, healthcare and labour power become commodities on the market. Rethinking economies through Māori perspectives may help to rethink the directions we wish to take in transforming our own lifeways.

The following is based on work we have done with Ngāi Tahu. We acknowledge that these ideas may not necessarily apply to other iwi, or even to Ngāi Tahu at different times. Tā Tipene O'Regan and Michael Stevens both argue that a key feature of indigeneity is the capacity for radical adaptation. Things change across time, or even across seasons and areas. These concepts were never fixed and static, and never will be, because Māori are protagonists in their own stories. In addition, many of these ideas are based on observations recorded by Pākehā after contact. This means they may be coloured by a Pākehā lens, and during this time Māori would have continued adapting and innovating.[7] These interpretations do not represent an untouched, pre-colonial state. Instead, they reflect evolving economic structures and ways of organising. One final caveat is that this is not a comprehensive account of every aspect of pre-colonial Māori economies. We are selecting aspects we see as useful, and setting aside those we see as not useful for informing possible futures.[8] These useful aspects, especially the ones that have endured through colonisation, could be keys to unlocking alternative economic futures.

Obligations, rights and resources

Obligations

The basic social and economic units for Māori were whānau (extended family), which could number up to thirty people. These consisted of three generations: kaumātua (elders) who stored knowledge and mentored; adults; and children. Hapū consisted of a number of whānau and were significant political units. Kāinga (villages) were fundamental to economic, social and environmental organisation. In some cases they still are, and in many they can be again. They vary greatly in size and population depending on resources and geography, but are places of living and organising together to meet the needs and aspirations of communities. Kāinga are not just villages but symbolic statements of mana over surrounding whenua, anchoring tangata in whenua as assertions of mana over whenua.[9] Paul Tapsell summarises the importance of kāinga for Māori lifeways as kāinga = tangata + whenua + taonga (resources). Tangata need to be in balance with whenua, to balance mauri (life force).[10]

Iwi are traditionally a temporary, large and unstable kinship collective formed to manage a crisis. They emerged as dominant institutions after colonisation because of the internal need to unify, and external Crown pressure to negotiate with larger groups.[11] Iwi are confederations of hapū that come together to defend the realm.[12] They are the sum total of constituent hapū, which are themselves an aggregation of whānau, and these are all bound together by whakapapa (genealogy).[13] These larger formations were possible within, but not necessary to, successful Māori economies prior to colonisation.

Obligations were typically organised around the two key aspects of life: tangata and whenua.[14] These were governed by a web of interrelations, always seeking balance guided by mauri, whakapapa and mana.[15] All aspects of life were anchored to the environment hapū lived in and moved across.[16] Economic and social relations were intertwined with the physical environment, which acted both as inspiration and limitation for these relationships. Food, clothing, tools and arts were all drawn from the land, to the extent that significant parts of the land, like mountains and rivers, shared kinship through whakapapa with those who were sharing its produce. This created a complex web of obligations and interrelations. Every craft and food production process contained a number of regulatory practices to acknowledge the importance of these natural ancestors in providing sustenance. The more important the practice to life, the more regulatory forces there were. Tohunga (experts) played a key role in balancing the energy of kāinga through whakapapa as a knowledge system that constantly builds on and rebalances existing knowledge with new knowledge to come up with innovative solutions to problems as they present themselves.[17]

Three key concepts are mana, mauri and tikanga. Mana is about one's rights and obligations. Mauri is the essence that exists in all living things. Tikanga is a set of normative ethics, broadly defined as Māori law, that specifies the correct or just behaviour in a given situation. In relation to natural resources, compromising the balance of mauri of the river, for example, damages not only the mana of the hapū that draws from that river but also its ability to subsist with the river. Mana, mauri and tikanga are linked because the wellbeing of the land is intertwined with the wellbeing of the people. Culture, therefore, steps in to keep pace with the environment as a co-determinant of the society's reproduction, or economy. Mauri connects obligations between people to obligations between people and non-human nature. In the context of Māori economies, exercising mana to balance mauri according to tikanga is a central motivation.

In Māori economies kinship was woven through economic groupings so that it exerted comprehensive economic functions. Obligations between people are best understood through the concepts of whakapapa and mana. Whakapapa connects all living things, past and present, and encourages individuals within a kinship grouping to make decisions against individual self-interest in favour of the collective progress of the whānau or hapū. An individual within a hapū is obliged to meet economic responsibilities because of social relationships that are difficult to undermine in the existing circumstances. Economic cooperation was achieved more easily when members of a working group shared kinship ties, strengthening their obligations to one another to achieve common aims. The binding forces of the social world were deployed to enhance production in the economic world. While this is also true of capitalism, that system demands both productivity and efficiency of production, including treating certain inputs as free and driving down the 'cost' of others. In Māori lifeways, productivity and efficiency of labour were not the point. Māori lifeways were not determined by the profit imperative. Obligations were enforced by a careful attention to both tradition and public opinion.

Reciprocal obligations tied people together in place to achieve economic aspirations within environmental contexts.

Rights and resources

Many authors have suggested that Māori had no concept of ownership. This assertion is problematic, because a narrow definition of land ownership obscures complex and layered perspectives on relationships between people and the rest of nature.[18] An absence of the concept of individual fee simple ownership does not equate to an absence of resource rights. Ūpoko Ngāi Tūāhuriri, Professor Te Maire Tau, argues that a key distinction between Western notions of property and Ngāi Tahu land rights is that 'land could not be alienated outside the tribe without tribal permission'.[19] Land itself was not 'owned' as such, but different resource areas and rights on land and in water were held by individuals, whānau and hapū through a complex array of rights dependent upon whakapapa, mana and occupation of an area.[20] Throughout the South Island, areas of land were separated into mahinga kai (food areas) which were specific to whānau, the rights to which were held by family elders. They may be thought of as more like resource user rights than ownership. These resources were defended fiercely, and individual and collective conflicts often occurred over resource rights.

Taonga resources are connected with rights and obligations, and provide a link between past, present and future generations. They encourage collective responsibility over individual rights, and evoke awareness of attributes which have incomparable and immeasurable values. The concept of taonga was fundamental to resource management practices, exchange and distribution, and labour. Different resources in different areas involved different sets of rights and obligations, exchange and distribution, and labour relations. Social sanctions also worked to enforce regulatory concepts such as rāhui (prohibitions) and mana. Although these regulations emerged from obligations to nature and ancestors, they manifested in practices that were enforced by the power of public opinion. Ignoring a rāhui could lead to light or serious reprisals (such as ostracisation) from others in the same community or an external community, and the social nature of this tradition ensured its enforcement on top of spiritual forces. Rights and obligations were intertwined with mana, which was enforced by public opinion.

People, land and resources were bound together by whakapapa, and this carried significant obligations. Taonga thus created relationships between people in place. Resources were relations.

A lot of research has been undertaken to confirm and advance the importance of leadership in Māori economies.[21] The role of rangatira (leaders) in upholding rights was significant, as land and water were extensions of the rangatira's mana. For example, in the Ngāi Tahu tītī economy, tītī (muttonbirds/sooty shearwaters) were so prized that strict user rights according to whakapapa had to be retained through continued usage, but could be given or removed at the discretion of the ariki (high chief with executive authority).[22] These rights were utilised collectively by whānau but belonged to each family elder. Operational authority lay with heads of whānau for their particular tītī island, while executive authority lay with the ariki to determine usage rights and tītī exchange. There was a hierarchical structure within Ngāi Tahu, but because authority and exchange were reciprocal and dependent on mana, it is likely that the arikis' executive authority enabled them to control exchange for both personal and collective benefit.[23] Leadership controlled the means of production and therefore the means of reproduction, but these leaders were held to account by their people in all aspects of the economy. Mana enabled rangatira to exercise influence and authority but was its own regulatory force, because mana had to be earned and maintained.

Exchange and distribution

Exchange

Even a superficial look at pre-colonial Māori society would suggest that trade of goods and services was extensive.[24] Pounamu (greenstone) made its way from a relatively remote region in Tai Poutini in the southwest to Te Tai Tokerau in the far north, and everywhere in between. Items frequently exchanged included coastal food and goods for inland foods and goods, and vice versa. All across the Ngāi Tahu region, different communities had access to different resources and therefore means of reproduction. The people of Wairewa and Waihora produced and distributed eels, Ngāti Waewae produced and distributed pounamu, the people of Kaiapoi produced kōura and kūmara.[25] Kaiapoi Pā, the tribal headquarters and central pā in the South Island, was built for the purpose of producing and distributing goods. The name itself refers to the swinging (poi) of food (kai) in and out of the pā – and is a metaphor for the trade that occurred among Ngāi Tahu at Kaiapoi.[26]

We follow the lead of John Reid and others who explore Māori exchange through the concept of tauutuutu, which places on individuals and communities an ethical obligation that emphasises balance, reciprocity and symbiosis in social and environmental relationships.[27] These relationships result in an ongoing cycle of mutually beneficial reciprocal exchanges. Tauutuutu stands in contrast to the imperatives imposed by capitalist markets, where the ability to pay for commodities, and inability to access necessities of life outside of markets, determines quality of life.

Goods were exchanged within and between whānau and hapū. In these exchanges, tauutuutu was driven by mana and tikanga. Exchanges created and reinforced obligations; and return exchanges, while potentially delayed, were of equal or greater value. This maintained the mana of each party in the exchange. Manaakitanga, broadly understood as hospitality, means to give mana. Leaders had to protect and grow their own mana, which required them to gift and lavish hospitality on others to increase their own status. Failing to behave altruistically would diminish their status as host, and ultimately erode their mana.

This also operated at collective levels, when a group hosted another group. In contrast to simple barter, which involves some sort of agreement in value or rate of exchange, exact values were not determined. Haggling was not considered appropriate, because bargaining diminished mana. Exchange was pragmatic, typically to attain resources from another area, and had a positive influence on status. This resulted in a sort of dynamic equilibrium, with mana driving exchanges that were ongoing and escalating, because an exchange created and maintained a relationship between giver, receiver and respective social groups. Delays in reciprocation ensured long-term relations were maintained, and bound groups together.

Tauutuutu also guided exchanges between humans and nature, and mauri was once again central. All exchanges needed to maintain or enhance the mauri of both parties because mauri can be enhanced or depleted through interactions. Balance was achieved when interactions were mutually beneficial, which helped distribute different resources across different regions. While it was an economic exchange, it was also a fundamental ethic that shaped behaviour and guided relationships between people and nature. To summarise, we quote John Reid and co-authors in full:

> Tauutuutu, at a basic level, can be outlined as escalating reciprocal exchanges that create and maintain social obligation and dynamic equilibrium as determined and regulated by mana and mauri and conducted within a web of whakapapa.[28]

Distribution

Distribution is about the sharing of surplus generated by the activities of a community, within that community. Understanding distribution requires both exploring the actual arrangements for dividing up the surplus between those who directly or indirectly created it, and the ideas governing these arrangements. The wellbeing of the community is directly influenced by distribution, and is therefore fundamental to understanding Māori lifeways. The 'mode of distribution' is located within the 'mode of production', providing incentives to work, ideas of equity, cooperation in production and planning for the future.

In Māori economies, as with all other things, distribution was bound by tikanga. Precise regulation was absent, and distribution was flexible across particular situations and varied according to public opinion. While land was 'held' collectively, and rights were organised individually, usually under the executive authority of the leader, resources were often supplied by individuals. Within a household, an individual made their contribution to a collective supply and then drew on this according to relative need. Reciprocity was relied upon to ensure the effectiveness of systems.

In large-scale projects, resources could be provided by the rangatira, who effectively shouldered 'risk', but the rewards from this outlay would not be considered 'interest' or 'profits' for that same leader. Rather, the reward was the creation of an object of social value to be utilised by the community, though this does not mean groups were immune from inequalities. The motive here was an increase in the mana of the leader, and manaakitanga again was fundamental to fuelling Māori economies. It was not about securing some sort of asset for minimal cost, but instead giving goods freely to people with the expectation that they reciprocate with work and loyalty. Distributions were also made to visitors as part of collective undertakings if they happened to be around. This was about politeness and respect for guests, but also increased the mana of hosts.

As far as distribution of the surplus from large-scale collective endeavours was concerned, the control of this usually rested with leadership or someone appointed by leadership. Whakapapa, manaakitanga and related responsibilities held these leaders in check, mitigating the potential for injustice and corruption. Leaders were required to pay attention to the interests of all, and public opinion could hold them to account for unfair distributions. The inability to accumulate massive stores of wealth also constrained the ability of leaders to insulate themselves from criticism. Although leaders did have a lot of authority, and could employ persuasive oratory, community consent was required for such activities, and distribution can be broadly described as 'delegated executive authority of persons of rank, held in check by public opinion'.[29]

Although it is inappropriate to force Māori concepts into strict alignment with the historically specific economic institutions we now know, many of the ills of today such as starvation and homelessness were unlikely in one family while others in the same village were living in abundance. Storing and saving food and other resources was common and necessary for both insurance against unproductive seasons or adverse events, and for meeting social obligations such as funerals or hosting visiting dignitaries. The moment of appropriation in capitalism, the point at which it is decided who claims the surplus, is structured into the capitalist state through forms such as contractual rights and private property. This appears to separate the economic from the political by normalising capital's claim to surplus. Māori economies operated within a completely different set of cultural and socio-political institutions. They were driven by the accumulation of mana, which was intrinsically reciprocal. One accumulated mana through the distribution and exchange of surplus goods.

While there were inequalities between rangatira, 'commoners' and 'slaves' in pre-colonial Māori society, no one was very rich or extremely poor in a relative sense.[30] Distinctions were based on relationship to the means of production and reproduction – the rights and resources discussed above – but exchange and the distribution of the surplus from these rights were governed by particular obligations. Prized ornaments and food delicacies did accrue to rangatira as manifestations of their mana, but though the quantity and value of these items might be considerable, their value also corresponded with the size of the leader's community. This relationship was not one-sided; the mana of rangatira was dependent on the respect and prestige they held with their people, which in turn relied upon how they treated those people. This created constant calls upon the resources of leadership, and the sources of wealth available to them corresponded with serious liabilities. This resulted in a sort of balance. A leader was never the sole possessor of accumulated wealth, yet a great deal of wealth would flow through their hands. While this did circulate to maintain a leader's mana, it also enhanced the mana of their people. In this way a leader's economic position was buttressed by their social status.

Distribution is tied in with mana, where mana is attained from how much passes through one's hands rather than how much accumulates in one's hands.

Labour and reproduction

The concept of labour is central to our exploration, but to date there has been little research on pre-colonial Māori labour relations. Labour carried dignity in Māori society, and the differences between labour and work (wage-labour) are central to many of the common misunderstandings about Māori labour relations. The alienation of workers from the products of their labour, as required by wage-labour, was fundamentally at odds with Māori labour relations. Large undertakings required all to share in labour, with rangatira working shoulder to shoulder with others.

Much day-to-day labour was, however, individual, spurred along by rivalry to win the approval of others. And producing a thing of quality – for instance, a carving to hold, gift or exchange – filled individuals with a strong conception of self-worth. Despite these individual motivations, unity within the group was undoubtedly very strong, and the claims of the group on the individual were rarely denied.[31] In the absence of false scarcity such as that imposed by capitalism, individuals freely contributed to collective stores without considering the exact equivalence of work in its commodity form. Their motivation was a sense of duty and the bonds that tied individuals to groups. Whakapapa was woven through economic groupings so that, in essence, kinship groupings drove economic activities. Above and beyond the incentive of public approval of individual work were collective responsibilities – contributions to collective wellbeing – and these were supported by custom, habit and tradition.

How a society organises the socially necessary labour required to reproduce itself is central to understanding that society. In Māori economies, respect for labour, not blind homage to work, helped to maintain social cohesion. Labour was considered honourable, and no one was demeaned by engaging in it. Even the highest leaders did not lose mana for engaging in labour (hence the contemporary expression 'tea towel tanga', which requires one to do the work to get the treats). While the dignity of position could remove a person from 'degrading' occupations, it was not a free pass for a life of leisure. Competent and confident engagement in labour was an important attribute for increasing influence and authority in communities, and the dignity of labour went hand-in-hand with disapproval of laziness. Community opprobrium of anyone thought to be neglecting their obligations is evident in numerous whakataukī; for example, hōhonu kakī, pāpaku uaua; (deep throat, shallow muscles).[32]

A tūao, similar to a working bee, is when a group of people get together voluntarily in a collective task, usually related to agriculture. For larger-scale activities, like net fishing and construction, the coordination of labour was tighter otherwise individual effort was wasted. In these cases, customary obligations and practices welded workers together. Firth provides an account of a work song, with leader and response, that helped in the paddling of a large waka.[33] Work songs increase the efficiency of collective production because energy use is more efficient if synchronised. Rhythm enables coordination of individual effort. Movement, words and participation also divert attention from strain and relieve fatigue. Songs improve cheerfulness and solidarity, and stimulate physical energy.[34] Māori perspectives on work, woven together by whakapapa as a form of kinship beyond solidarity, rejected the alienation of labour. For the most part, you got out what you put in, but this was mediated by obligations and forms of exchange.

The fruits of Māori work were not alienated. They did not sell their time to someone else who owned the means of production and received some portion of the value generated in that work through a wage.

Conclusion

In this chapter we have explored existing interpretations of how pre-colonial Māori economies may have been organised. We suggested that land, water and resources were (and are) taonga, and their use was organised around a complex web of kinship rights and obligations based on whakapapa. Land and resources are socio-ecological relations. We also suggested that exchange was based on reciprocal obligations between people and place to maintain and enhance mana and mauri. Mana was therefore an engine of the economy.

Surplus distribution was often controlled by executive authority but this was held in check by public opinion. Distribution was also regulated by tikanga according to mana, because mana is enhanced by how much passes through one's hands rather than how much accumulates in one's hands. Finally, we suggested that work was both individual and collective when required but was not alienated, as happens when the fruits of an individual's work are extracted and workers are compensated with a wage. Leaders played important roles in all of these features of the economy, but were held to account at all times by fierce participation and public opinion. Whakapapa and mana were therefore central to and determining of these key features of past Māori economies – obligations, rights and resources; exchange and distribution; and labour – and will be central features of Māori economic futures.

We have sketched out a set of principles that could be useful in charting possible economic futures, and we take this up in the final chapter. There are many more features in many more contexts that we could explore. In many cases, these features were deliberately undermined, restricted, erased and replaced through colonisation to make way for capitalism. But this was not the case from day one, and as we detail next, there are several periods in New Zealand's colonial history worth exploring to understand how we got here and where we might go next.

3. Stabilising a Colonising Economy

Early Encounters, Dispossession and Reparations

In this chapter we will briefly outline three key periods after initial contact that have implications for understanding Aotearoa's political economy. The first period is between European contact and the signing of Te Tiriti o Waitangi, and relies heavily on existing historical interpretations. The second begins in the 1830s but focuses primarily on the period after Te Tiriti/the Treaty and the dispossession of Māori economies to establish the bases for the colonial-capitalist economy. The third period is our contemporary neoliberal period, beginning in the 1980s, including modern Treaty settlements that have sought to provide some reparation for dispossession. Treaty settlements contain possibilities for future alternatives but have certainly created new contradictions. Overall our intention is to illustrate the evolution (sometimes gradual and at others rapid) from Māori choosing to engage on their own terms with commercial opportunities, to being subsumed by the capitalist economy and associated imperatives that were forcibly established. This is, at its heart, a story about land: the basis of any mode of production.

The unfulfilled possibilities of early economic encounters

The early encounters between Māori and Pākehā – that is, those that occurred in the broad period between European contact and the signing of Te Tiriti o Waitangi – ranged from violent to intimate, exploitative to mutually beneficial. There is no single story or set of ideas that can be taken from one area and applied to another. Following many others, however, we choose to emphasise Māori self-determination in these encounters. We do this because many histories position Indigenous peoples as those whom things happen to, rather than as protagonists in their own stories.

Critical histories have highlighted the violence of primitive accumulation to challenge histories that whitewash colonialism. This whitewashing usually stresses the 'civilising' effect of Europeans, or assumes colonisation was inevitable. Both views obscure Indigenous self-determination. Māori have always and will always make active decisions about how they engage, or refuse to engage, with the forces of the international economy, though this is not always in conditions of their own choosing, with autonomy being stripped away over time. In early encounters with colonising forces, some Māori turned away and some saw opportunities that they embraced. This will continue. Crucially, early economic encounters occurred on Māori terms, and were incorporated into existing Māori economies and relationships.

These encounters are noteworthy because they suggest possibilities of what could have been if systematic colonisation had not occurred, or at least if Te Tiriti had been even partially honoured. These encounters demonstrate a 'before' that encompasses different methods for organising life which might have evolved in many possible directions. This reinforces the distinction between contact and colonisation, and the fact that capitalism is neither natural nor inevitable. Early encounters varied greatly according to the resources, timing, exposure, internal politics and other factors in each area.

Because people tend to stress the differences between Māori and Pākehā, now and then, we can sometimes overlook the similarities.[1] Trade and barter (forms of commerce but not necessarily capitalism) were key aspects of early encounters. Māori ceremonial gift exchange continued through engagements with Pākehā, but more utilitarian exchanges that were commercial in nature also continued and expanded. Some Māori clearly demonstrated a willingness to establish ongoing relationships with Pākehā, and others merely wanted specific goods and one-off transactions. Although these exchange relationships were complex, an eagerness to trade, secure a bargain and develop enterprise was demonstrated clearly by Māori from contact.[2]

Hazel Petrie explores Māori economic development prior to and immediately following European contact in *Chiefs of Industry*.[3] Petrie describes how Māori expanded the production and trade of traditional goods to gain the maximum benefit from trade opportunities, but also took on new products and processes. These included provision of fish, pounamu, timber and flax, as well as sealing, whaling, and the growing of potatoes and wheat. Many of these activities were carried out according to old ways and new means.[4] That is, Māori were able to incorporate new productive activities into existing social relations, so that they maintained existing patterns of rights and resources, exchange and distribution, and labour, even as they were beginning to engage with the international economy. By this point the vast majority of commercial opportunities were mercantile trade. Kāi Tahu historian Michael Stevens follows Marshall Sahlins to suggest that the first commercial impulse of Indigenous peoples is to become more like themselves rather than becoming European. For us, this suggests that these early commercial opportunities and technological advances meant that Māori could continue existing lifeways, and enhance mana, while incorporating diverse products and practices.[5]

New opportunities also created space for individuals within, against or beyond whānau, hapū and iwi collectives.[6] Sometimes these opportunities aligned with the aspirations of collectives, but sometimes they undermined them. Individuals could undertake their own exchange activities, begin to engage within a European property rights regime, and work for waged labour on ships or in other areas. In addition, these activities presented new challenges to resource management that pushed at environmental limits. At this point diverse economies were emerging, and people and groups moved between these practices on their own terms. The external relations and forces of the international economy began to impact on the internal organising of Māori communities.[7] Mana and mauri were undermined as determining of rights, exchange and distribution, and labour.

The resource-based nature of Māori economies and identity meant that Māori, and especially Kāi Tahu in the south, were mobile rather than fixed in place. Kāi Tahu archaeologist Atholl Anderson suggests mobility was (and still is) almost a defining characteristic of the southern people.[8] Michael Stevens takes up this argument, suggesting that on contact with Europeans, Kāi Tahu continued and expanded this mobility. They were active participants in social and economic mobility, using the Tasman Sea as a bridge rather than a barrier.[9] Not only did the arrival of Europeans eventually lead to a sort of peace between Kāi Tahu and Kāti Māmoe in the southern regions, but there was a gradual migration south of many Kāi Tahu to make the most of new opportunities offered by participation in the emerging economies. Stevens provides many examples of this, including the Weller brothers' shore whaling station. This was established by negotiating an agreement with local rangatira Tahatu, and secured by marriage to his daughter Paparu. This station mixed whaling, shipbuilding, farming, and the trade of flax, fish and preserved Māori heads, employing up to eighty-five people. This rapid change reshaped families, labour, consumption and production. It brought oars, sails, harpoons, wet-weather gear and oil lamps, among other things, but Kāi Tahu knowledge of weather, tides and whale migration patterns were the 'software' needed to make it all work.[10]

Kāi Tahu historian Angela Wanhalla and various co-authors have explored cross-cultural relationships in the early economies of southern New Zealand.[11] These were kin-based economies, with success tied to building relationships.[12] Ngāi Tahu built long relationships with shore whalers, enabling mutually beneficial access to resources, labour and other opportunities. These relationships often manifested through marriage between the Pākehā whalers and Ngāi Tahu women. Just as relationships built alliances pre-contact, these extended into the post-contact period, expanding out and into wider kinship networks. But they were more than trade alliances; these people forged intimate ties, including the benefits and obligations that came with joining Ngāi Tahu society.[13] Labour was performed by families, and surplus distributed back into family and community according to whanaungatanga (relationships) and manaakitanga. When the whales disappeared, the whalers remained.[14]

However, critical arguments and implications are hidden by focusing exclusively on possibilities and opportunities. There is an important distinction between a commercial opportunity and a market imperative. At what point do commercial opportunities become imperatives because alternative lifeways (beyond those of capitalist markets) have been extinguished? Initially, commercial opportunities were a choice to improve livelihoods, but eventually capitalist markets became a necessity to meet the basic needs of life. As sovereignty was extinguished and social relations were transformed, opportunities for Māori to become more like themselves turned into imperatives to become less like themselves and more like capitalist subjects.

There is no way of knowing the multitude of reasons why Europeans arriving prior to systematic colonisation from 1840 chose to come to Aotearoa. But the simple fact is that the conditions of the places they were coming from were miserable for workers.[15] During and in the aftermath of the Industrial Revolution the lives of working-class people were immeasurably worse than before.[16] Rural landholdings were being consolidated, commons were being enclosed, and people were pushed off the lands into overcrowded urban centres where living and working conditions were overwhelmingly harsh. The state and political institutions had yet to be reformed to provide collectivised forms of social security.[17] Far-off colonies like New Zealand presented possibilities that had become completely out of reach for workers in Britain. So they came to explore and find their fortunes. Some of them found happiness through other means, like marriages, loving whānau, and new ways of understanding and engaging with the world. But these newcomers were undoubtedly part of a large spatial fix. By 'spatial fix' we follow David Harvey to mean displacing the contradictions of capital in space and time; never resolving the dynamics causing the crisis tendency, but instead shifting impacts onto future generations or those at the margins of society who will be typically unable to do much about them. In Aotearoa, it was Māori who were marginalised by this process. Even so, it has been demonstrated over and over again that Māori have always and will always resist marginalisation, within, against and beyond existing constraints.

In Britain, capitalists actually had too much capital, and were running out of places to invest it profitably.[18] At the same time, workers and the poor were beginning to better understand their own conditions, and resolving either to leave those conditions or to try to change them. To quell the possibility of revolution, these people needed to be given new hopes and dreams that wouldn't threaten the status quo. Edward Gibbon Wakefield is very clear that his proposed fix for both an undersupply of profitable investment opportunities, and an oversupply of angry, potentially revolutionary workers, was systematic colonisation. It is this that we turn to next. Individuals arriving from Europe and engaging in the economy on (mostly) Māori terms was one thing, but the fix, 'the art of colonisation', required more: dispossessing Māori of their land, resources and ultimately their self-determining authority.

Primitive accumulation and the dispossession of Māori lifeways

The question of land is central to understanding the changing shape and control of Aotearoa's political economy. Land is the basis of all reproduction of people and economies. The processes by which Māori land and lifeways have been dispossessed and transformed into the bases for a capitalist economy have advanced in a number of stages across the nineteenth, twentieth and twenty-first centuries. This section deals with broad themes spanning the 1830s to the 1980s.

The dispossession of Māori land and lifeways begins as extra-economic power used to construct and maintain the conditions for economic power to operate. As Barbara Bradby explains:

> Capitalism's methods of destruction are three: force, the State and taxation, and the introduction of cheap commodities. Force is used because of the speed with which capitalism needs large-scale expansion of raw material production and increases in the labour-force. Exchange plays a role in the destruction of the natural economy but capitalism cannot wait centuries for a slow process of breakdown to be worked through. Pre-capitalist peoples may have no desire for exchange, in which case the only way of getting hold of their land and raw materials will be by force. Usually there is an alliance between political and economic factors which is necessary to break down processes of reproduction which are effected through a mixture of the political and the economic.[19]

The bases for the future capitalist state were first established via extension of the British Crown's authority to New Zealand, initially via New South Wales. This created the foundations of 'legitimate' extra-economic power, which would change over time into different institutional forms and functions according to the balance of class forces and their strategic engagement with the existing state. The Crown as early capitalist state exerted authority through violence, or the threat of violence, to reshape Aotearoa into settler New Zealand by establishing the conditions for colonial-capitalism. But over the decades, especially following the Second World War, outright physical violence became less necessary as the compulsions of capitalist accumulation took over. When the conditions for self-expanding value are established and alternative lifeways are extinguished or subordinated, capitalism takes on the appearance of being natural and inevitable.

In this way, the social forces coalescing in the early capitalist state used extra-economic powers to set up a framework in which economic powers would continue the process of dispossession. In this framework, Māori would no longer be able to blame the Crown, but would instead be blamed as 'uneconomic' agents for their own colonisation and dispossession. We suggest that continuing to situate the Crown as the primary enemy of Māori in colonialism has let capital off the hook.[20] Continuing to refer to the Crown without historicising its relationship to the capitalist state limits possibilities for decolonisation. Our view is that although 'the Crown' has evolved over time from the British Crown, to a Crown colony government, to a representative settler government, all are manifestations of the capitalist state – a set of social relations that secure the conditions for capitalism but that could be used to prefigure alternative conditions.

In this context, with newcomers becoming increasingly lawless, and the proliferation of problematic land deals based on speculative gains, a treaty between the Crown and Māori became necessary for a range of reasons. Much has been written on Te Tiriti/the Treaty, so we will not discuss it in detail here.[21] But several key points are worth noting. First, there are two versions: the te reo version (Te Tiriti) that the majority of Māori signatories signed, and the English version (the Treaty). Both contain three articles, but there are some fundamental differences between the two versions. In Article

One of Te Tiriti, Māori leaders give the Queen kāwanatanga, a transliteration of governorship. In Article One of the Treaty, Māori leaders give the Queen the rights and powers of sovereignty. Ranginui Walker points out that if Te Tiriti ceded 'mana', more akin to sovereignty than kāwanatanga, then it is very difficult to imagine Māori signing it away. Māori never ceded sovereignty.[22] Article Two of Te Tiriti guarantees tino rangatiratanga (unqualified chieftainship) to Māori leadership over whenua, kāinga and taonga (land, villages and resources), whereas the Treaty guarantees undisturbed possession of lands and estates, forests, fisheries and other properties. Article Three guarantees Māori the right and privileges of British subjects, and is considered the most accurately translated.

Te Tiriti effectively established *at least* dual economies by guaranteeing rangatiratanga over whenua, taonga and kāinga: that is, self-determining authority over land, resources and lifeways. But colonial-capitalism's insatiable need for the fundamental asset in the new political economy – land – trumped the benevolent or otherwise contractual obligations outlined in Te Tiriti/the Treaty, thus setting up the enduring contradiction at the heart of New Zealand.[23] The large-scale dispossession of Māori land was a genesis moment for capitalism in this place, and is unquestionably an example of primitive accumulation.

A great deal of very thorough research has already explored the dispossession of Māori land. Some of this dispossession has also been framed as a form of primitive accumulation.[24] The processes by which land has been dispossessed include the assertion of Crown pre-emption over land purchases; war and confiscation in the latter half of the nineteenth century; decisions of the Native Land Court; forced acquisition through state expropriation; and post-war regulatory changes.[25] In short, land was and still is the primary source of 'capital' for the New Zealand colonial-capitalist economy. Because it was in an *invaluable* Indigenous social form, not a valuable capital asset, it had to be dispossessed from one sphere to accumulate in another. The transformation of Māori lifeways was required for colonial-capitalist property relations to be secured.[26]

Pre-emption

The first wave of dispossession took place through Crown pre-emption. Te Tiriti/the Treaty established the Crown as the single buyer of Māori land. The Crown, as a colonial government, was thus able to secure and extend authority over vast swathes of Māori land for prices which would allow profitable on-sale as a source of public funds. This was necessary to establish a local form of capitalist state to aid the evolution away from the British Crown. By the mid-1860s the Crown had ownership of almost all of the South Island and significant sections of the North Island. Ngāi Tahu, in particular, lost control of the vast majority of their lands through Crown pre-emption. As the Waitangi Tribunal reported in 1991, 'the Tribunal cannot avoid the conclusion that in acquiring from Ngāi Tahu 34.5 million acres, more than half the land mass of New Zealand, for £14,750, and leaving them with only 35,757 acres, the Crown acted unconscionably and in repeated breach of the Treaty of Waitangi.'[27] The Tribunal referred to this as Ngāi Tahu being in 'Wakefield's laboratory' for colonisation. Simon Barber extends this framing to establish Ngāi Tahu's land loss as a form of primitive accumulation, concluding that Ngāi Tahu were effectively made to fund their own colonisation.[28]

Catherine Comyn argues that it was the British capitalist class, rather than the British Crown or settler government, that provided material support for early colonisation. The New Zealand Company's *Tory* set off on its maiden voyage without sanction and in direct defiance of the authority of the British Crown. Comyn points out that prior to the *Tory* even landing in New Zealand and its passengers negotiating land purchases with Māori, 110,000 acres of Māori land had already been 'sold' by the New Zealand Company. It was pure and rampant fraud. The New Zealand Company thus occupied a paradoxical position where reckless speculation was required to keep it afloat but was also driving it towards collapse.[29] The company ended up heavily indebted. With so much and so many invested, one of the first orders of business for the newly established New Zealand Parliament in 1854 was to authorise the public bailout of the New Zealand Company: 'It was thus that the founding of the modern nation of "New Zealand" quite aptly coincided with the settling of its colonial debts.'[30] In this way, the interests of the Crown and Wakefield's New Zealand Company, that had been at odds during the 1830s and early 1840s, found commonality. The British Crown's projection of authority was absorbed into the representative settler government via social forces on the ground.[31]

Keith Hooper and Kate Kearins have found that between 1840 and 1859, Crown purchases of Māori land for resale at a higher price made up a significant portion of Crown revenue.[32] The low prices paid by the Crown for Māori land were justified by the assumption of ephemeral or normative benefits for Māori, like 'civilisation' under British rule. British expectations of economic growth in New Zealand were based on Māori land cheaply acquired and later appreciating in British hands. Already by 1844, £4,054 had been paid for land that was sold for £40,263. However, because the New Zealand Company's vision of systematic colonisation resulted in rampant and fictitious speculation, far fewer settlers showed up to work the land than anticipated. This frustrated agricultural and infrastructure development, and led to unemployment, because it prioritised speculation which thwarted investment in production.

While Crown pre-emption was put forward as a mechanism to protect Māori from dodgy speculators, in reality it protected dodgy speculation and was central to financing systematic colonisation.[33] Through monopolising control over the forms of human–nature relations such as the construction of private property and the distribution of land or territory, it also established the foundations of the capitalist state in Aotearoa.[34] This was the key to Wakefield's art of colonisation. He argued that land (capital) was so abundant (after being dispossessed from Indigenous peoples) that labourers would not work for a wage when they could obtain their own land and work it themselves. He was not supportive of establishing a new subsistence economy outside of the capital relation in New Zealand; the goal was a capitalist economy to meet the needs of British capital. Because the supply of labour was not constant, regular or sufficient, it would always be uncertain. This meant dependence of the labourer on the capitalist must be artificially created, and Wakefield suggested that the way to create this dependency was to put an artificial price on the 'virgin soil', independent of supply and demand: '[I]n the business of settling a new country, the mode in which waste or public land is disposed of by the government, must necessarily exercise an all-important influence'.[35] This also offered the new colony an early source of financing. So not only was Wakefield's art of colonisation about dispossessing Indigenous peoples, it was also about funding the settler government and installing a capitalist class system in the new colonies:

> Capitalists brought up in this country do not like to work with their own hands: they like to direct with their heads the labour of others. The necessity of working with their own hands is apt to disgust the emigrant capitalist, and to send him back to this country a discontented and complaining man.[36]

This was, explicitly, colonial-capitalism. In this way, then, Te Tiriti/the Treaty was an attempted extension of the extra-economic power of the Crown, clearing the way for the foundations of economic power to be established by the turn of the century. We should make it clear that we are not suggesting the perfect alignment of historical actors like the Crown and the New Zealand Company. Rather, we want to illustrate how groups advance their own interests through the capitalist state. In this case, capital was able to advance colonisation for accumulation, initially in defiance of the Crown and later with its support.

Although a lot of Māori land was sold through contracts, some if not all of these contracts occurred with violence, or the threat of it, as the backdrop. For example, overt Crown violence against Ngāi Tahu did not occur in the large purchases of Te Waipounamu for a number of reasons, but the threat was imminent. And it was certainly threatened by Kemp aboard the *Fly* in Akaroa Harbour in 1848. When Māori in the North began to refuse to sell their land, and started organising collectively against dispossession, the threat manifested into an extended campaign of violence. Raupatu or the violent confiscation of land was the settler government's alternative. Hazel Petrie argues that by this time settlers had a confidence derived from knowing they could call on the empire to support their interests. By 1860, the combination of this, the settler hunger for land and decreasing Māori willingness to sell culminated in war in the central North Island.

Raupatu and violent seizure of land

Māori resistance to the ongoing advance of land-hungry settlers erupted into the violence of the land wars throughout the 1860s in Taranaki, Tauranga/Bay of Plenty, Waikato, Hawke's Bay and Te Urewera. Eventually the Crown, by now a representative settler government, passed legislation to confiscate land from those Māori deemed to have been involved in rebellion. This confiscated land, well over 3 million acres, included some of the most promising areas for the forms of pastoral farming that would later emerge as dominant in New Zealand.[37] Its seizure from Māori was devastating to the communities whose ability to reproduce themselves relied upon their relationship to the land. Indeed, it was no coincidence that wheat plantations and mills were specifically targeted for destruction by the Crown forces because these not only enabled Māori to reproduce themselves but were also a threat to the ascendant colonial-capitalist economy.[38] Much has been written about the land wars.[39] Here we reiterate the point that when Māori began refusing to sell land, it was instead confiscated: the next mechanism for dispossession.

The Native Land Court

Following seizure of land through pre-emption and outright physical violence, a more insidious form of dispossession emerged. First, Crown pre-emption was slowed by Māori resistance to land sales, which required the Crown to advance raupatu and confiscation to continue dispossession. Eventually the Crown abandoned exclusive pre-emption in favour of both private and Crown purchasing. The Native Land Court, first established by the Native Lands Act 1862, was designed to transform Māori relationships with land into private property rights within the emerging capitalist political economy. This advanced the breaking down of communal forms of tenure and the drawing of Māori into capitalist property relations that were started with Crown pre-emption. In great part, the solidifying capitalist property regime and violent removal of fertile lands from Māori created a situation whereby selling further land in order to access the means to live was for many the only option. The effect was devastating and highly divisive for whānau and kāinga.[40]

Effectively, the court granted tenure of Māori land to individuals or smaller numbers of owners. Many of these individual owners then became indebted through survey and legal fees. In the context of an emerging and unavoidable predatory market economy, the only way out of debt and to make ends meet was to sell land. Between 1861 and 1891, Māori land holdings in the North Island reduced from 22 to 11 million acres.[41] While pre-emption was rapid, and raupatu through war and confiscation was brutal, the Native Land Court effectively undermined the mana of Māori individuals and communities. In many cases the court turned them against each other. The consequences were insidious and demoralising. In particular, the ability of individuals to enter into sales contracts meant that the mana of the rangatira, based on reciprocal obligations, was drastically undermined. Rangatira still had all the obligations of their positions, but were unable to command the resources to meet those obligations. This was a huge blow beyond direct land loss for Māori economies, because it disrupted the intimate relations between tangata and whenua, mana and mauri, that drove the lifeways described in Chapter Two.

A 'kind' kind of dispossession

With the three processes outlined above, the vast majority of Māori land was expropriated. But there was still more to come, and much of this dispossession occurred beneath a seemingly sympathetic political veneer. Despite the Liberal government openly regretting past land dispossession and sympathising with Māori between the 1890s and 1910s, Māori land was still acquired through the Native Land Court during this period, and compulsorily acquired under several Acts. Again, land was acquired and then later resold at a considerable profit. Exorbitant survey fees, government commissions and local government rates exacerbated land loss. This dispossession in one sphere towards accumulation in another was often justified as being for the public good. In effect, it was to ensure a continuous flow of revenue for the Crown.

During this time, governments oversaw a decrease in Māori land ownership from 30 per cent of land in 1890 to 7 per cent by 1912. A lot of this land went to a new class of small farmers, often on favourable long-term leases rather than by sale.[42] In the meantime, Māori were still disproportionately funding the settler government. The Reform administration that replaced the Liberals in 1912 also undertook a systematic programme of purchase. By 1930, approximately 3.5 million more acres were lost to Māori, with Māori land holdings diminishing to just 3.6 million acres. Much of this remaining land was inaccessible backcountry and unsuitable for agriculture.[43]

Successive governments of this time and many since illustrate the hypocrisy and technocracy of liberal dispossession. Instead of employing the direct violence common in previous decades, and in other colonies, lands and lifeways were confiscated through 'objective' accounting and other techniques used by experts to demonstrate 'poor returns' and 'waste lands' as a justification for acquisition.[44] This harks back to the Lockean doctrine used throughout the colonial-capitalist world of the moral imperative to 'improve' land – 'improve' meaning to make as productive as possible. Even so, the government was heavily indebted for much of this period, and had a declining international reputation for creditworthiness.[45] While Māori land underwrote both the government and the settler economy, both remained weak.

In the period following the Second World War, Māori continued to be dispossessed by government under a liberal veneer. Te Maire Tau argues that the combination of the Town and Country Planning Act 1953 and the Maori Affairs Amendment Act 1967 resulted in a mass migration of Māori from rural land which they owned to urban areas in which they predominantly had to rent.[46] The Town and Country Planning Act meant Māori land could be re-zoned as rural; as a result, only one house could be built on approximately 10 acres. Māori land holdings were too small and dispersed to be commercially viable and too externally constrained to be residentially viable. Furthermore, these Acts reduced the capital value of the land. Under the Ratings Act 1967, local councils, which in any case often failed to provide sufficient services to Māori land holders, could sell Māori land when rates were unpaid. Such losses had the dual effect of making cheap Māori reserve land available for the predominantly settler agricultural economy and causing Māori to move into cities to provide labour for the predominantly settler industrial economy.

In addition, Paul Tapsell argues that after the Second World War the psychological pain of returned Māori war veterans at not receiving a war pension, despite their having fought for the coloniser; and then having to labour for a wage on alienated whenua given to returned Pākehā soldiers, triggered trauma and struggles with alcoholism and domestic violence. This had flow-on gendered impacts despite mana wāhine keeping fires burning at the kāinga.[47] Tapsell continues that the individualisation of wages was the final step in the assimilation of Māori into the colonial-capitalist economy.[48] Wages subverted the aspects of Māori economy associated with kāinga through further urban migration. Wages created status, provided an escalator out of rural isolation, and initially appeared to be a cure for the ills of colonisation.[49] But as we know, the colonial-capitalist economy is subject to boom and bust, intervention or lack of intervention, and class struggle.

Neoliberalism hit Māori workers hard, and when the wages dried up, kāinga had been all but emptied. Even as the use of extra-economic powers to dispossess Māori became frowned upon as New Zealand progressed, the conditions were created for economic powers to continue dispossession and ramp up proletarianisation (people having to labour for a wage to survive). Neoliberalism emerged in the 1980s as a re-articulation of the capitalist state, and provided huge gains for capital (protecting and expanding private property) but large losses for people (reducing spending, social support and union membership).

While land has been the focus of this and most other histories, it is worth noting that many aspects of Māori lifeways were facilitated by water – including mahinga kai and transport.[50] When mahinga kai were fenced off, dammed, drained or polluted, Māori were cut off from many lifeways. The Crown's environmental policies, at best relaxed, at worst deliberately destructive, have had a role in this, as has the fact that water is essential for agriculture. Broadly, these related processes of fencing, damming, draining and polluting have been likened to Māori lifeways as an 'externality sink' for the capitalist economy, which needs sources to produce all of its goods and sinks to dump all of its ills.[51] Māori lands and lifeways were often the victims of this externalising machine. Destruction of mahinga kai, land loss, and the inability to take up pastoral licences, meant that Māori were cut off from both traditional economies and the ability to participate in the new settler agricultural and pastoral economy.

Dispossession of Māori land is by no means the only change that negatively affects Māori economies and autonomy. Hazel Petrie describes a complex dynamic that brought about sudden declines in Māori economic power. This dynamic encouraged settler acquisition of Māori land on one hand, and was exacerbated by the loss of land and collateral by Māori on the other. The colonial-capitalist project encouraged and incentivised Māori to concentrate on wheat growth, flour mills and ships. This narrowed focus and restricted flexibility when local and global market conditions required it. The longer-term impacts of this, still escalating today, are that socio-ecological reproduction is also undermined through specialisation and monocultures, leading to soil depletion, deforestation, water degradation and so on. Loss of land meant loss of collateral, and servicing existing debts to meet the basic needs of life for individuals and communities exacerbated land loss. The land wars, Native Land Court, and antagonistic shifts in government policy that either negatively affected Māori or positively favoured Pākehā, took up Māori time and energy. To this day, significant Māori money, time and energy is put towards defending rights, resources and rangatiratanga, rather than using rights, resources and rangatiratanga to advance wellbeing. Although Māori had initially embraced local and global market economies, the combination of settler hunger for land and the imperatives and volatility of these markets had a devastating effect. Land loss was not the sole basis for Māori economic troubles, but land loss certainly represents a 'final death blow' to Māori dominance in the New Zealand economy.[52]

In sum, over time the economy of mana, particularly the mana of the rangatira, was undermined. Land was dispossessed, but so was the mana of Māori as a key regulator and driver of Māori economies. Without land, and with diminished mana, Māori were excluded from the new settler economy while their economies were being erased. Without resources within capitalism, and without alternatives beyond it, Māori were gradually forced into waged work. Rights and resources were dispossessed so work, exchange and distribution were drastically changed within a few generations. However, while understanding the loss of Māori land is central to understanding New Zealand's political economy, recognising the economic aspects of land loss is insufficient for understanding Māori economies. Land is a relationship, and land is life.[53] In te reo Māori, whenua is both land and placenta, and the whenua (placenta) is buried in the whenua (land) to maintain kinship connections in and with place. Both Simon Barber and Paul Tapsell stress the relationships inherent in the expression 'tangata whenua' – tangata meaning people, whenua meaning land – and highlight how the processes above have slowly transformed the relation of tangata and whenua into labour and property.[54] In this way, the mana of mana whenua was undermined by transforming whenua into property. This change drastically altered resource rights, the executive authority of rangatira, the mana of exchange and distribution practices, and labour relations. But this transformation was never and will never be complete. As early as 1849 Ngāi Tahu were voicing their dissatisfaction with land loss, and these and other struggles coalesced in modern Treaty settlements, which we turn to next as a particular contemporary manifestation of Māori economies.

The possibilities and contradictions of Treaty settlements

Modern Treaty settlements are manifestations of Māori struggle within and against colonial-capitalism. We think of them as reparations rather than full and final settlements. Lots of people from across the political spectrum have had lots to say about Treaty settlements, but it's worth writing off, right now, the ahistorical and frankly racist critiques of settlements as a 'gravy train'. The total value of finalised settlements is estimated at only $2.2 billion between 1993 and 2018 – a tiny fraction of the $1,322 billion of overall government spending in that time, and in the vast majority of cases settlements represent a tiny fraction of what was lost.[55] Nor, as Matthew Wynyard points out, have there been substantial returns of Māori land as part of the Treaty settlement process.[56]

Though settlements come under constant critique, Māori have put a great deal of intergenerational effort into pursuing a better future for their descendants. We want to acknowledge this effort, and the fact that it has resulted in better lives for many within current conditions. Ngāi Tahu, in particular, take their role in struggling for Te Kerēme (the Claim) across seven generations very seriously. Te Kerēme was born in 1849 when the first formal statement of Ngāi Tahu grievances against the Crown was made by Matiaha Tiramōrehu.[57] From 1849 to 1998, Ngāi Tahu fought relentlessly for the resolution of grievances through any means possible.[58] This included a case with the Native Land Court in 1868, a royal commission of inquiry in 1879 (the Smith–Nairn Commission), another royal commission in 1886, and the 1921 Native Land Claims Commission, all of which supported Ngāi Tahu's claim with varying effects and compensation. None of these was deemed sufficient. Although these processes were largely subject to the political whims of agents of the Crown, the Claim was carried across generations and each additional process gathered evidence of Crown wrongdoing. Te Kerēme effectively became a key aspect of Ngāi Tahu identity, expressed through this intergenerational protest against the broken promises of the Crown.

The core tenets of Te Kerēme were: the failure to reserve adequate land for the iwi; unjust prices paid for land; unclear boundaries of purchased land; failure to provide schools and hospitals; and restricted access to mahinga kai.[59] Te Kerēme was an important manifestation of self-determination for Ngāi Tahu.[60] Te Tiriti/the Treaty, land purchase contracts and now the settlement create ongoing responsibilities and obligations between the Crown and Ngāi Tahu.

Details of the contemporary settlement are outlined in the Ngāi Tahu Claims Settlement Act 1998, and the story of the negotiations and settlement is explored in Martin Fisher's book *A Long Time Coming*.[61] The settlement was to provide an economic base for Ngāi Tahu reconstruction. In this way, it may be considered a reparation.[62] In addition, part of the settlement process resulted in the Te Rūnanga o Ngāi Tahu Act 1996 which, among other things, recognised the independent legal personality of Te Rūnanga o Ngāi Tahu, which has a constitution that is not subject to political interference by the Crown.[63] The settlement consisted of various forms of redress, including:

- land and cash (nominally valued at $170 million, but also including major bolt-ons);[64]

- access to mahinga kai;
- co-management of certain conservation and resource management processes;
- exclusive ownership of a mineral, pounamu – a taonga for Ngāi Tahu;
- recognition of place names (e.g., Mt Cook became Aoraki/Mt Cook);
- an apology by the Crown.

We will discuss the good work that has been done with this settlement in the next chapter, and some of the tensions and contradictions that it has raised. But there are also valid critiques from Māori about the reality of Treaty settlements as an expression of rangatiratanga and economic self-determination, and about the underlying intentions of the Crown.

The current form of these reparations emerged right in the midst of neoliberalism, and although they have evolved over time and are not all uniform, the maximum quantum of the reparations can be traced back to the fisheries settlement.[65] The pan-Māori fisheries settlement is often referred to as the Sealord deal, and was signed in 1992, setting the maximum available in any single settlement at $170 million.[66] Simon Barber draws connections between the Crown purchases, subsequent colonial policy, the settlement of grievances, and the resulting form of post-settlement governance entities (PSGEs) and Wakefield's systematic colonisation. In Barber's framing, Ngāi Tahu's PSGE structure is a continuation of colonisation, with the corporatisation of the iwi supported by the breakdown of traditional structures.[67] Ani Mikaere conceptualises the assimilative thrust of Treaty settlements as the trading of a profound relationship with land and sea for cash to achieve ends that are both assimilatory and divisive, at the same time creating structures that will prevent further rangatiratanga in the future.[68] Michael Stevens argues that settlements have simply reinscribed the existing power culture, and that whether Māori economic power might translate into autonomy and independence in the long term is unclear because options are structurally constrained.[69] Paul Tapsell describes 'iwification' during the modern Treaty settlement process, arguing that the concept of iwi was legislatively appropriated beyond its customary context. The Crown's privileging of large iwi, bunching together hapū, has in some ways drowned out the voice of kāinga. The entities that have emerged – the PSGEs – create new Treaty partners for the Crown that effectively strip the rangatiratanga from rangatira and hapū in relation to their whenua, kāinga and taonga.[70] These critiques of modern Treaty settlements and the structures that emerged suggest a reduction of 'rangatiratanga' to financial autonomy. But the movements that coalesce around these critiques pressure both the Crown and PSGEs to push back against this reduction.

Professor Margaret Mutu and collaborators have conducted an ambitious and comprehensive research project to interview Treaty claimants and negotiators.[71] In the papers from their study so far, Māori report being subjected to ongoing injustice in the negotiation and settlement process because of the divide-and-rule approach taken by the Crown. Some report being bullied into accepting government-determined settlements, given a lack of room for negotiation; vast inequalities in resourcing between negotiating parties; conflict around confidentiality, which is anathema to Māori society and incompatible with expectations for leadership; and a chasm between Māori and Crown expectations of settlements. According to Mutu, the process is better referred to as a 'Treaty claims extinguishment process' rather than a Treaty settlement process. This is because rather than seeking to restore the honour of the Crown and right the wrongs of the past, the government's specific intent was initially to unpick legal rights won by Māori in the Lands case of 1987; to extinguish all historical claims; and to preserve European control over Māori lives.[72] However, Mutu writes, '[F]or Māori, existing "settlements" are not full, not fair and, in contradiction to the pronouncements of governments, not final.'[73]

Despite these profound and far-reaching critiques of modern Treaty settlements, they are often accepted for pragmatic reasons in the short term, with the expectation that in the long term more progressive change can be advanced by Māori.[74] *Matike Mai* (discussed more fully in Chapter Five) explores and supports opportunities for constitutional transformation, putting forward the 'spheres of influence' model – with a kāwanatanga sphere, a rangatiratanga sphere and a relational sphere – in which a Te Tiriti relationship will operate.[75] This framework has since been taken up by many authors, activists and leaders.[76] However, the economic implications of spheres of influence and constitutional transformation have been less explored, and we will ask some preliminary questions about these in Chapter Five. In the next chapter, we will take a look at what Ngāi Tahu have done with their reparation. This is not necessarily to defend Treaty settlements against the critiques above, but to acknowledge the pragmatic approach that Ngāi Tahu and other Māori leaders have taken in playing the long game. In doing so, we also point out some of the contradictions that arise with the economic effects of Treaty settlements.

Conclusion

The structure of colonialism in Aotearoa was set in motion on the other side of the world, not just by a handful of individuals who wished to spread religion, or as an inevitable development in the progress of humanity, but as the result of the compulsions of capitalism which require ongoing expansion. Colonising forces met and for decades existed on the terms of Māori lifeways, before attempting a violent extension of an alien 'sovereignty' across the land and people. This sovereignty, or extra-economic power, is the reverse of economic power, which is the system of laws and authorities by which private property, formal labour rights and systems of production and exchange are asserted and enforced. Here, the lifeways of Māori political economy which spring from established relationships to Aotearoa, and which are reflected within but do not draw originating authority or power from Te Tiriti/the Treaty, are placed in perpetual struggle against the totalising (but never total) social relations imposed by capitalism.

The enforced transformations of existing Māori relationships to reflect, for example, definitions of legal ownership of land within the capitalist system of private property, changed the appearance but did not destroy the pre-existing Māori economies in their entirety. This partial transformation from one mode of production to another will remain incomplete as long as the sovereign basis of a Māori political economy remains to contradict the dominance of colonial-capitalism.

4. Diverse Economies in Aotearoa

Māori Businesses or Māori Economies?

> What is the relationship of this capital to this culture? ... We have ... a substantial disconnect between this intergenerational dream of a Ngāi Tahu heritage and identity, and the economic structure we have established to fund it.[1]

Here Tā Tipene O'Regan asks the question confronting all Māori organisations, economists and activists today. He is referring specifically to Ngāi Tahu, but the question can be asked more generally: how is capital related to a particular culture? How are Māori to engage with capitalism into the future? To address this question we will explore the contemporary development of Te Rūnanga Group, the organisation; and Ngāi Tahu, the iwi, and all the related layers of whānau, hapū and kāinga. These are often conflated by those unfamiliar with the iwi, but they are interdependent, not synonymous. We argue that the distinction between the organisation and the iwi reveals the pivotal moment that we are in. Although this is a single organisation and iwi, many of the lessons could be useful for other iwi and Indigenous peoples struggling within, against and beyond colonial-capitalism. Not every lesson here applies to other contexts, but many may.

The dominant framing of the 'Māori economy' does not explicitly distinguish between Māori businesses in the colonial-capitalist economy and Māori economies battling against and beyond this. It also fails to recognise the diversity within and between Māori economies.[2] We distinguish between a colonial-capitalist economy with Māori businesses in it, structured according to the profit imperative, and Māori economies built on Māori practices and perspectives that are not structured in this way.[3] While exploring Māori autonomy and perspectives *within* and *against* colonial-capitalism is essential, the focus here is on the transformative potential of Māori economies *beyond*, which is less well understood.

Te Rūnanga Group – the organisation

Te Rūnanga Group emerged as neoliberalism was shattering Māori and many other communities in Aotearoa. The organisation was based both in *and* against neoliberalism. Neoliberalism benefited Te Rūnanga Group, at the expense of Ngāi Tahu whānau and kāinga.[4] It did so because the organisation was established to receive the settlement assets.[5] Many of these assets didn't exist prior to neoliberalism but were privatised as part of the rapid fire sale of state assets throughout the 1980s and '90s.[6] Property rights were created where there were none previously. These property rights could then be claimed as part of the settlement process.[7] In Aotearoa, neoliberalism is used loosely, usually to refer to a set of ideas or an ideology, without being situated in relation to global capitalism. It needs to be recognised as an ideology that maintains capitalism.[8]

Te Rūnanga Group was established by Ngāi Tahu elders to protect their grandchildren from the hardship they were facing under neoliberalism and that a previous generation had faced in the Great Depression.[9] These crises keep coming around and disproportionately impact Indigenous, minority and working people. They occur because of the contradictions inherent in capitalism. The vision of the elders was that the corporate form would be temporary, and that the settlement was about rebuilding the marae and surrounding kāinga. The marae and kāinga could maintain their own rangatiratanga, coming together when necessary as an iwi to 'defend the realm'.[10] This response illustrates that Māori have enduring social forms that can improve their lot within capitalism (while stabilising it) but also hold possibility beyond it (prefiguration). But the corporate beneficiary form is still very much here and in some ways has entrenched economic and political authority in the organisation at the expense of the kāinga. How this organisation benefits present and future generations of Ngāi Tahu people and groups depends on how these people and groups reassert their mana and rangatiratanga.

Organisational structure

The structure of Te Rūnanga Group is quite complex.[11] It has four key parts: Papatipu Rūnanga (similar to local councils); Te Rūnanga o Ngāi Tahu (the board); the Office of Te Rūnanga o Ngāi Tahu; and Ngāi Tahu Holdings. This structure was designed to incorporate the 'best corporate governance models we could find in the world and draws from the democratic structures of local government and Western best practice' and 'embraces our cultural traditions'.[12]

Eighteen regional Papatipu Rūnanga exist around the Ngāi Tahu region to uphold the mana of their people over whenua. Papatipu Rūnanga also deliver benefits from Te Rūnanga Group distributions at the local level. Each has unique opportunities and challenges presented by the tangata and whenua of their specific regions. The eighteen Papatipu Rūnanga elect appointment committees, who in turn appoint representatives to Te Rūnanga o Ngāi Tahu. Te Rūnanga o Ngāi Tahu is effectively a board or overall council of Ngāi Tahu representatives responsible for the governance of Te Rūnanga Group. Te Rūnanga o Ngāi Tahu issues annual Letters of Expectation to the Office and Holdings, and these units develop Statements of Corporate Intent establishing how they intend to fulfil those expectations. Therefore, it is essential that processes are put in place to ensure that the different needs and aspirations of individual Papatipu Rūnanga are heard at the table. This raises a contradiction in that individuals are representatives of their Papatipu Rūnanga, but as council members are trustees of the collective resources of the iwi.

Te Rūnanga Group's assets are managed by Ngāi Tahu Holdings, separately from the body that spends and distributes a portion of the income earned from those assets, the Office of Te Rūnanga o Ngāi Tahu.

This feature of the post-settlement structure has been criticised as restricting self-determination because it maintains top-down authority for decision-making, despite sometimes being led by Ngāi Tahu individuals.[13] It also maintains a rigid dichotomy between 'culture' and 'commerce', where culture is upheld by the Office and kept separate from commerce, which is managed by Holdings. In this way, cultural accountability and commercial accountability have been separated. This has traditionally resulted in a focus on maximising profit for distribution rather than alternative approaches that might seek to build value in an encompassing way. But this is changing over time to meet the broader demands of the iwi.

Ngāi Tahu Holdings is divided into business units that focus on intergenerational investment according to their maxim; 'mo tatou, mo ka uri, a muri ake nei' (for us and our children after us). This requires an investment strategy ensuring growth that at least matches but should outpace growth in the Ngāi Tahu population. Under-investment or over-distribution today can be an injustice towards future generations, but over-investment or under-distribution today can be an injustice towards present generations. All of these strategies and decisions must be in line with the aspirations of the past seven generations that fought for the claim. At the time of writing, Ngāi Tahu Holdings portfolio sections are Farming, Forestry, Property, Seafood, Tourism, Oha Honey and Investments. The basic idea is to diversify activities as much as possible to develop intergenerational investment and the ability to weather the challenges and contradictions of the global economy. This 'diversified portfolio' is said to have allowed Ngāi Tahu Holdings to survive both the 2008 financial crisis and Covid-19 – though not without significant job losses, distribution reductions, asset sales and revaluations.

Most of the work that is done within the organisation is waged labour. In many cases this supports Ngāi Tahu people by paying them to do work they would otherwise not be paid for. However, this wage relation can distort obligations away from kinship and towards the employer, creating complexity when these obligations do or do not align. Likewise, most of Te Rūnanga Group's activities operate as part of capitalist markets, though there are areas where gifting practices and reciprocal exchanges based on tikanga endure. Distributions are organised along a corporate beneficiary model, with Holdings providing an overall distribution to the Office, which then distributes to Ngāi Tahu individuals and collectives. Some distributions are equality driven, some are equity focused, others are whakapapa based, and some prioritise ahi kā — those who have kept the fires burning in the kāinga. The property relation is not traditionally capitalist because there is not a clear distinction between those who own the means of production and those who do the work. The primary 'shareholders' or beneficiaries are Ngāi Tahu, including those not yet born. While this intergenerational investment also exists more generally in contemporary capitalism, Te Rūnanga Group prioritises distant future generations. This results in longer-term intergenerational investment than occurs in typical capitalist firms, illustrating how Māori ways of organising enable this sort of organisation to do capitalism well and, to that extent, stabilise it.[14]

Te Rūnanga Group was set up to receive many of the settlement rights and resources. This causes conflict, as many at the kāinga level see the central organisation as an extension of the dispossession of their rights as mana whenua. While the characteristics of Te Rūnanga Group make it difficult to draw exact comparisons with other organisations, it most closely resembles an extension of the capitalist state – with a crucial caveat. Some have argued that the Treaty settlement process has created PSGEs in the Crown's own image.[15] However, so long as Te Rūnanga Group continues to draw its authority from rangatiratanga, rather than from an assumed and illegitimate claim to sovereignty as the Crown does, it has a more legitimate claim to sovereignty. Although it can be argued that Te Rūnanga Group derives its authority from legislation in the kāwanatanga sphere (e.g., Te Rūnanga o Ngāi Tahu Act 1996), the charter of Te Rūnanga o Ngāi Tahu establishes a collective repository of rangatiratanga. And the charter is independent of the Crown, so that this authority can only be maintained with the consent of whānau, hapū and kāinga.[16] Because of this, it works in some ways to stabilise capitalism but also contains seeds of possibility to prefigure and reconstruct Māori economies beyond it. This raises, once again, our stabilisation or prefiguration argument, which we return to in Chapter Five. In sum, the organisation occupies a space within and against colonial-capitalism while assembling the tools to build beyond. To be very clear, the organisation was designed to inhabit capitalism, and in this it has done well. But it has taken a pragmatic approach to pursuing rangatiratanga through the conditions set by the capitalist state, while maintaining possibilities beyond.

Distributions

With mostly pragmatic investment and shrewd use of settlement mechanisms, the 1998 settlement of $170 million has grown into 'tribal equity' or 'net assets' valued at $1.71 billion.[17] A portion of earnings are continually transferred from Ngāi Tahu Holdings to the Office for distribution – $55.9 million (with a $240 million net accounting profit) in 2020–21 and over $689 million since settlement. Although priorities for distribution come and go depending on responses to crises (financial crises, earthquakes, housing crises, pandemics), distributions outside of crisis response tend to be at three levels of development – whānau, rūnanga and iwi.

Around the time of settlement, hui were conducted with Ngāi Tahu whānau, including youth and elders, and staff, to discuss aspirations and establish what the iwi wanted to look like going into the future. Out of this emerged *Ngāi Tahu 2025*, which provided a road map for aspirations, strategy, investment and distributions.[18] Subsequent progress reporting is supposed to be measured against this document, so that it provides an important mechanism for whānau to hold the organisation to account. Tā Tipene O'Regan discusses three important themes around investment and distribution:

sustaining identity, social spending and defending the realm. He questions what the point of any of this wealth is without rebuilding and developing Ngāi Tahu culture, identity, wellbeing and self-determination.[19]

Sustaining identity

> If Ngāi Tahu want to be a tribal nation, if we truly want to own ourselves, we have to own our own memory.
> – Tā Tipene O'Regan[20]

Te Rūnanga Group has funded reconstruction of Ngāi Tahu identity since settlement. This includes archives, mapping and place names, language and whakapapa. In 2020 the Ngāi Tahu archive was co-located with Archives New Zealand at a specialist facility in Christchurch.[21] These collections are managed by the iwi but the co-location provides an opportunity to partner with the Crown and share resources. The archive is crucial for ensuring that current and future generations can maintain access to Ngāi Tahu history and knowledge. The archives also develop online resources and books so that the iwi can access this knowledge now and in the future.[22] This open access means that settlement resources are being used in ways that are non-excludable and non-rival – they are open and do not deplete as they are consumed. One of these resources is Kā Huru Manu, the Ngāi Tahu cultural mapping project, which records and maps Māori place names and associated histories in the Ngāi Tahu area. Much of this is accessible to the public and therefore provides a shared resource for all to better understand Ngāi Tahu and Te Waipounamu.

Kotahi Mano Kāika, Kotahi Mano Wawata (One thousand homes, one thousand aspirations) is the iwi language revitalisation strategy. This focuses on the intergenerational transmission of te reo Māori through a range of initiatives and resources for all levels of learners. In 2020–21 there were 746 whānau actively engaged in Kotahi Mano Kāika, including 90 new participants.[23]

The whakapapa team is ensuring the tribal register is accurate, so that members can provide or be provided with evidence of their whakapapa connections. The team often provides the first information for Ngāi Tahu seeking to reconnect, and maintains the integrity of whakapapa records at an iwi level. As of late 2021, there were over 71,000 registered Ngāi Tahu iwi members, with 3,868 new enrolments during the 2020–21 financial year.[24]

Finally, a significant portion of distribution goes directly to Papatipu Rūnanga development, much of which is invested at marae level, and contributes towards reconstruction – physical and metaphorical – of Ngāi Tahu marae, kāinga and related institutions. This gives those rūnanga – who keep the home fires burning – the autonomy to determine how they use those funds, and these are generally increasing over time so that the marae and kāinga can grow with and then beyond the central organisation. All of these activities and more are about revitalising individual and collective identity. In this case, distributions from the capital are supporting the reconstruction of Ngāi Tahu identity. The possibility remains that as identity is reconstructed, there is potential for asserting that identity as a sovereign body with a material base beyond colonial-capitalism. Te Rūnanga Group was designed to inhabit capitalism, and is working through it to construct possibilities beyond.

Social spending

The second area for distribution is social spending, which Tā Tipene refers to as 'subsidising the benefits of citizenship' that Ngāi Tahu are entitled to under Article Three of Te Tiriti, and as tax and ratepayers. These attempt to fill the gaps left by the inequities of colonisation and the collapse of collective reciprocal obligations within the kāwanatanga sphere under the capitalist state. But they also seek to develop capacity beyond colonialism.

The concurrent Covid-19 pandemic and housing crisis has meant more focus on these emergencies as part of spending distributions. This includes shared equity homeownership schemes, significant health spending, and emergency response capability led centrally as well as at rūnanga level.[25] This emergency response capability was developed during the Canterbury earthquakes of 2010 and 2011, and was able to swing back into action for the pandemic in 2020, but was always based on enduring practices of reciprocity.[26] Many aspects of rangatiratanga have been obscured by kāwanatanga and colonial-capitalism. But when there is a shock to colonial-capitalism – like an earthquake or a pandemic – that reveals its shortcomings in serving human needs, ruptures emerge for rangatiratanga to bubble through and reveal itself as an enduring alternative. And while Te Rūnanga o Ngāi Tahu and Ngāi Tahu are our focus, rangatiratanga has been asserted all across Aotearoa, including in Covid and cyclone relief, distributions and checkpoints, as well as urban Māori authorities caring for all. Since Te Tiriti, rangatiratanga has always existed with an alternative and more legitimate claim to sovereignty than the Crown-as-capitalist state, ignoring or deliberately breaching its Te Tiriti obligations. An alternative state exists, and while both are currently subordinated to the capital relation, one contains decolonial possibilities grounded in Māori lifeways.

Whai Rawa was established within Te Rūnanga Group for Ngāi Tahu whānau to benefit directly from the settlement, and to encourage savings that can be used for education, homeownership and retirement. Te Rūnanga funds the operations of Whai Rawa, matches savings to a certain amount, and makes direct distributions. The scheme has more than 31,765 members and manages over $123 million in funds.

Education has made up a large part of Te Rūnanga Group's social spending since settlement, with a number of scholarships available at all levels of education, as well as other forms of education spending, direct programmes to build capacity such as cultural competency, and leadership and governance programmes. Tokona Te Raki, a Māori futures academy, is creating capacity among rangatahi to confront a rapidly changing future. Though this is a form of social spending, it also sustains identity, and defends the realm by building intergenerational capability. All of this spending, however, is reliant on the success of Ngāi Tahu Holdings, and its distribution, as it navigates the boom and bust of the crises of capitalism.

Defending the realm

An important feature of the centralised nature of Te Rūnanga Group is that it can invest considerable resources in defending the realm. This was a key feature of pre-colonial and pre-settlement iwi as a federation of hapū uniting to defend borders.[27] Boundary and other legal challenges took up a significant amount of Te Rūnanga Group and the wider iwi's efforts during the first ten years post-settlement.[28] These included blocking boundary disputes from other iwi in the northern parts of the South Island through court challenges. While initially creating difficulties for pan-iwi development in the South Island, these antagonisms have largely, although not entirely, been put aside.[29]

Te Rūnanga Group devoted considerable resources to struggling against the Foreshore and Seabed Act 2004, including involvement with a campaign to urge members of Parliament to vote against the legislation and a submission to the UN Committee for the Elimination of Racial Discrimination (CERD). The CERD found that the legislation discriminated in its extinguishment of the possibility to establish customary title, and urged the government to resume engagement with Māori.[30] Te Rūnanga Group has also been fundamental to the Christchurch rebuild and has devoted resources to legislative and regulatory changes, including enabling papakāinga developments on reserve lands.[31] It also has groups working on internal and external strategic challenges, including engaging with the Crown, the Resource Management Act and Treaty settlement issues. It develops internal policy on issues such as how to preserve taonga assets that have use value to Ngāi Tahu whānau, and climate change adaptation and mitigation strategies.[32]

Court cases and experts are expensive, but the centralised settlement resources enable Te Rūnanga Group to support this expenditure to defend and advance Ngāi Tahu rights. This builds institutional capacity in the rangatiratanga sphere. These and other initiatives have attracted and will continue to attract support from outside Māoridom too.

These are all examples of Te Rūnanga Group defending the realm within and against the capitalist state. The capitalist state is able to facilitate ongoing dispossession of Indigenous land, lifeways and self-determining authority through colonial hierarchies of recognition (the Foreshore and Seabed Act and degradation of freshwater are prime examples). The role of centralised iwi agencies in defending the realm is often underplayed in critiques of post-settlement governance entities. These critiques do, however, make important points about the blurred line between protecting Indigenous rights and protecting economic interests.

Tensions and contradictions

When a large group of people is brought together to plan for, manage, grow and distribute a centralised resource in perpetuity, there can be tensions as different aspirations collide. There have long been tensions about how Ngāi Tahu Holdings conducts its business in line with Ngāi Tahu values; and whether it is the right vehicle to control collective resources, some of which are taonga. There can also be tensions around distributions. The most pervasive of these is the cost of distribution: how much does it cost Te Rūnanga Group to distribute each dollar to members? And who decides and delivers distribution programmes – the Office, Papatipu Rūnanga or whānau? Underlying all of this is a constant tension between having a strong centre (Te Rūnanga Group) and strong regions (whānau, marae, kāinga), where mana and rangatiratanga sit. Some see the centralised Te Rūnanga Group as a barrier to their tino rangatiratanga; others see the eighteen Papatipu Rūnanga as a part of that same system preventing mana motuhake-a-hapū/whānau (independent authority of hapū and whānau).

While many acknowledge this capitalist accumulation as a success, others argue that the model has financialised aspects of Māori land, bodies, lifeways and self-determining authority, transforming the layered collectives of Ngāi Tahu whānau, hapū and iwi into individual Te Rūnanga Group beneficiaries. This disenfranchises and limits the authority of hapū, whānau and kāinga both within and beyond colonial-capitalism. But the organisation and the iwi are not the same thing. The use of the term 'Ngāi Tahu Whānui' to mean the collective public of Ngāi Tahu individuals also creates conflict. Some argue that the central organisation creates a one-way relationship of dependency, rather than a multitude of layered relationships based on reciprocal obligations as organised in whānau, kāinga, hapū and iwi. This model transforms active citizens organising in autonomous kinship and geographical associations into passive beneficiaries.[33] Capitalism requires centralisation and scale, and this drives the consolidation of power that many within the iwi take issue with. Te Maire Tau has recently stated that the organisation was designed in the 1990s to deal with 1990s problems, and that this structure has been replicated by many iwi since. But these structures may not be fit for existing and future problems, so they need to be redesigned.[34]

These tensions build on the core issue, which is actual sovereignty over land and lifeways, and the different ways this sovereignty might be defined (for example, according to capitalist imperatives, or not). Matthew Wynyard points out how little land has actually been returned as part of Treaty settlements.[35] Much of this small amount of land returned to Te Rūnanga Group has been repackaged and sold off again as residential property to maximise financial returns. This short-term profit-maximisation, driven by conventional incentives, could have significant long-term consequences for the mana of Ngāi Tahu. It might lead to an over-accumulation of financial capital at the expense of the mana and whenua that is the basis of the mana whenua status. Some argue that maximising of Ngāi Tahu hapū land held is paramount and urgent because of its intrinsic use value and ability to nurture Ngāi Tahu lifeways. Others see the issue as one of timing, arguing that using market forces in the present and generating financial exchange value through those forces will enable more land holdings in the future.[36] This example exposes the contradiction inherent in a clash between colonial-capitalist value and Indigenous values, where tensions between use and exchange value are leading to a future in which Ngāi Tahu might 'be rich and landless'.[37] Tā Tipene O'Regan suggests that this could be acceptable for a conventional investment trust but never for an Indigenous people seeking to restore their authority within the settler-state, and notes 'a substantial tribal groundswell against this trend'. This also highlights the difference between land as an asset and whenua as a relation, and reveals the way that the capitalist state maintains capitalist relations through the enforcement of private property rights.

One response to the iwi-led critiques around the sale of land for profit is for Ngāi Tahu Holdings to work the land in ways that make it financially viable without on-sale. Ngāi Tahu Property developed Ngāi Tahu Farming, which subsequently invested heavily in dairy farming. While there are aspirations to do dairy better and provide leadership for others to follow, the reality is that in the current market conditions it is difficult to achieve this within environmental limits that the iwi and many others consider acceptable.[38] Charlie Mitchell details a conflict between Ngāi Tūāhuriri (a hapū of Ngāi Tahu) and external parties around opposition to a resource consent for a Canterbury irrigation scheme on the grounds of cultural offence. He writes: 'For some Canterbury Māori, the agricultural pressures on the environment have gone too far, which has pitted two world views against each other: One in which rivers have mauri (a life force), and one where rivers are resources that can support a community's economic livelihood.'[39] The difficulty lies in the fact that although Te Rūnanga o Ngāi Tahu and Ngāi Tūāhuriri opposed the development, Ngāi Tahu Farming was a shareholder in the scheme. Here, instead of selling off land, the organisation is pursuing profit, which in capitalism requires polluting upstream from the mahinga kai and related lifeways of whānau and kāinga. In the meantime, Ngāi Tahu - the iwi as a whole - is often blamed for the intensification of dairying despite many in the iwi and mana whenua opposing the activities of the organisation. In Chapter Three, we noted that Te Maire Tau describes Ngāi Tahu mahinga kai and other lifeways as an 'externality sink' for the settler economy. In this case, the organisation is externalising its economic activities into the subsistence activities of the iwi.[40] He argues that the system needs to change before those inside it can change, because the profit motive will always constrain the best of environmental intentions.[41] It is very hard to operate outside of global capitalism, and it is very hard to be good inside it.

But, as always, none of this is total or inevitable. The reason these tensions and others like them exist is because Te Rūnanga Group is merely the tip of the iceberg. Too often Te Rūnanga Group and the organisations within it are used as synonyms for Ngāi Tahu. But the iwi is layered and complex, scattered throughout the world, with Papatipu Rūnanga spread across the diverse landscape of Te Waipounamu. As whānau, marae and kāinga are being rebuilt from the ravages of colonisation, often resourced by the activities described above, they are exercising their own rangatiratanga. Rangatiratanga is where alternative futures lie.

Ngāi Tahu – the iwi

When thinking about contemporary Indigenous economic development as a particular but not total expression of self-determination, it is crucial to differentiate between Indigenous corporations and Indigenous kinship groupings. They are interdependent but not synonymous. It is at the marae, kāinga and whānau level that the fires have been kept burning. Those fires are getting stronger and stronger, particularly with activities like mahinga kai, and pounamu harvesting and carving, that have endured at the boundaries of colonial-capitalism. We will explore some of these activities to illustrate opportunities and challenges for Māori economies.

John Reid and Matt Rout at the Ngāi Tahu Research Centre have conducted detailed then-and-now comparisons of particular Māori economies. In a recent study, they focus on activities around tītī and pounamu because these have long been central to Ngāi Tahu identity, and have evolved in complex ways with implications for rights, exchange and distribution, and labour. We rely here heavily on Reid and Rout's research, which is extensive, detailed and open access.[42]

The tītī economy

The tītī economy is often described as the only real Ngāi Tahu tribal economy, because it maintains Ngāi Tahu economic practices and institutions.[43] Tītī are a taonga for Ngāi Tahu, and are understood through whakapapa connections, creating obligations for kaitiaki. The annual birding season takes place between the beginning of April and end of May, and the activity is centred on a group of small islands near Rakiura/Stewart Island where tītī nest. Tītī are typically processed (plucked, salted and bucketed) on the island and taken to the mainland for distribution. Rout and Reid note that it is difficult to track the tītī economy, but it was already a significant operation by the time of European contact. Today harvests vary drastically across years, but buckets of ten to twenty birds sell for $200–$500, and 60,000–120,000 buckets are harvested annually.[44]

Both pre- and post-contact, the tītī economy has remained politically, economically and socially important. While the Crown negotiated the purchase of Rakiura, local Māori ensured that some tītī islands were reserved for harvesting.[45] The tītī economy therefore stands out from the conventional experience of settler-colonialism's erasure of Indigenous economies, as having been preserved and developed over time. The process, tikanga and a degree of rangatiratanga were maintained over some islands. Rout and Reid find that aspects of pre-colonial economic organisation have been maintained in parts of the tītī economy: it is still an important expression of cultural identity, whānau cohesion and tribal autonomy, and although new technologies have been introduced, the basic process of birding remains as it was. In addition, some practices that were almost lost are being maintained and revived as part of a broader Ngāi Tahu resurgence.[46] Tītī harvesting is still largely carried out at the whānau level, although employment in waged labour elsewhere makes it is more difficult to return to the islands for two months a year. Although rights to some areas are still based on whakapapa, and there is plenty of non-market mana-enhancing exchange, rights and exchange have still been affected by interaction with colonial institutions and the market economy.

Researchers at the Ngāi Tahu Research Centre and tītī harvesters together argue that the loss of executive authority associated with the mana of chiefly leadership means there is no single authority that can regulate exchange and adjudicate rights.[47] In terms of exchange, this leads to a situation where competition between whānau results in harvesting pressures, declining returns and the leakage of resources from whānau into the wider market economy. In pre-colonial exchange practices, leadership was able to regulate supply to benefit the collective and restrict individuals from undercutting one another. Today, excessive competition from the encroachment of market forces leads to downwards pressure on price, and gives more power to large buyers to 'clip the ticket'. This hinders the ability of whānau to cover the financial costs of the activity, let alone the social and ecological costs. It also results in less coordination, communication, collaboration and knowledge transmission, and this impacts whanaungatanga, tikanga and mātauranga (knowledge). In short, the tītī economy has been able to maintain many aspects of pre-colonial economic organisation through a particular assertion of rangatiratanga, but it is still subject to the competitive pressures of the market.

The pounamu economy

While the tītī economy illustrates some of the contradictions between traditional and market exchange, pounamu illustrates some of the contradictions between traditional and contemporary organisations. Pounamu is prized for its appearance and durability, was an essential part of traditional Māori society, and is an expression of Māori identity today. The name for the South Island, Te Waipounamu – translated broadly as Waters of Pounamu – demonstrates its importance. All pounamu comes from one geographic region, meaning it is particularly significant to Ngāi Tahu, Kāti Māmoe and Waitaha identity, and therefore to their history and pre-capitalist economic organisation. While it was spiritually prized, pounamu formed a crucial part of national trade as a mobile and highly prized resource. The mana of the carver was and is critical to the value of pounamu; that value is derived not just from where the stone is from, or how the stone was worked, but from who worked it. The designs are taonga that carry and transmit knowledge.

During the Ngāi Tahu purchases, Ngāi Tahu hapū from the West Coast insisted that they maintain their rights over and access to pounamu, and were given assurances that this would be the case. These assurances were not honoured, and much pounamu harvesting and carving knowledge has been lost. Pounamu rights were returned in 1997 as part of the Ngāi Tahu claim. While this led to some celebration, there were tensions around whether the right to harvest, labour, exchange and distribute the surplus pounamu should be managed in Christchurch by Te Rūnanga Group or whether it should remain with the local hapū and kaitiaki who had maintained these practices and obligations.

This issue of centralisation versus decentralisation is another contradiction in contemporary Māori economies. Traditionally iwi did not necessarily claim ownership over and collectively *work* resources; rather, they combined to defend rights from external threat. Individuals, whānau and, when necessary, hapū worked resources. But now iwi both own property and work it, sometimes at the expense of the autonomy of mana whenua. How, then, can the mana of kaitiaki and carvers be maintained in this new pounamu economy, given that there are still external threats to the resource?

Tremaine Barr and John Reid outline a resolution for this contradiction – a Symbiotic Development Model.[48] They point out that external threats to the pounamu economy include a substantial black market for illegal pounamu that Te Rūnanga Group is now required to monitor and police in light of the Crown backing away from regulation. And while this monitoring and enforcement infrastructure was being organised following settlement, a substantial amount of jade from overseas was imported.[49] 'Ownership' remained with Te Rūnanga Group, but the responsibility for resource management plans was devolved to kaitiaki rūnanga to better match traditional structures of authority and rights. In this scenario, kaitiaki rūnanga practise customary and commercial pounamu extraction and manufacture; while Te Rūnanga Group provides regulatory authority and some economies of scale for exchange and distribution. Key to guarding against external threats is traceability to establish authenticity, and this guarantee of authenticity also adds significant value.[50]

The Symbiotic Development Model, which was developed over a substantial period with broad participation at various levels of Ngāi Tahu, from carvers to executives, supports a centralised (state-like) infrastructure maintained by Te Rūnanga Group, and decentralised commercial management of pounamu at whānau and rūnanga level. Barr and Reid call this 'centralised decentralisation'. The model enables Ngāi Tahu pounamu to resist market imperatives to reduce costs and prices because of the ability to coordinate distribution and trace authenticity. This authenticity can emphasise the tapu, mana and mauri imbued in each piece, enabling a prestige price. This compromise has shortcomings, and some Ngāi Tahu carvers have opted out of the system to maintain their own mana.[51] But the system allows for the protection and sustainable management of pounamu while enabling whānau and rūnanga to exercise their rights in a form of self-determination. The organisational structures and rights of colonial-capitalism have challenged Indigenous economies, but there are ways around these, or at least compromises within them. These compromises require committed participation, collaboration and mana-enhancing development strategies.

Conclusion

Although both the tītī and pounamu economies have endured in some ways, have maintained some aspects of the economy of mana, and are resurgent, they are still forced to engage with colonial-capitalism and its institutions. This raises contradictions with regard to rights, exchange, distribution and labour that have to be negotiated or overcome. In view of this tension, there has been a general move towards aligning the aspirations of whānau, kāinga and Papatipu Rūnanga with the central organisation. This alignment includes autonomy for decision-making around local issues, including financial autonomy for investments and distributions. Many of the Ngāi Tahu Papatipu Rūnanga are a long way from economic centres, with limited access to work and housing. Recently Te Rūnanga Group has established a regional development fund to enable Papatipu Rūnanga to lead their own localised or kāinga-centric outcomes for their people, with support from the centre. It is creating conditions for alternatives within a central state-like form, in much the same way that the capitalist state created the conditions for small farming in the late nineteenth century. This approach focuses on job creation, social inclusion, economic multipliers (thinking about how value bounces around an economy rather than staying focused solely on distributions), environmental and cultural sustainability. The fund is about 'lighting 18 fires', with an emphasis on capability-building for rūnanga.[52]

The mana and rangatiratanga of Ngāi Tahu is grounded in whānau, hapū and kāinga, not in Te Rūnanga Group.[53]

The organisation was established as part of the settlement process, and many Ngāi Tahu within and outside of the organisation are rethinking its design in the contemporary context, especially in respect of maintaining and enhancing the mana and rangatiratanga of whānau, hapū and kāinga. This has been supported by the material base received as part of settlement, managed and grown by Te Rūnanga Group. In addition, urban Māori authorities have established spaces of rangatiratanga within cities and other areas, and are developing alternatives, working within, against and increasingly beyond the limits of the kāwanatanga sphere and colonial-capitalist economy. Despite this, the cases described above that have managed to endure through colonialism still have to confront the colonial-capitalist economy.

This raises a key argument to be taken forward into Chapter Five. The reality for Māori seeking to maintain or reconstruct Māori economies is that it is impossible to remain fully outside of capitalism because of its global dimensions and expansionary dynamic. And it is impossible to 'do good' within capitalism because of its constructed scarcity, the tendency for the profit rate to fall and the imperatives of the market. If Māori are to be the agents of economic change, those changes will emerge from scaling up these spaces of rangatiratanga.

5. Alternative Economies are Possible

Economic Transformation and Questions for the Future

The question that inspired this book is: what are the economic realities and possibilities of decolonisation in Aotearoa? This is a layered and nuanced question, with layered and nuanced answers. In this short book we have been able to engage only with some possibilities, but our purpose is to build on existing conversations and initiate new ones. This final chapter focuses on three key arguments and concludes with more questions. The first key argument concerns the boundary struggles between colonial-capitalism and Māori economies, or the stabilisation versus prefiguration dynamic. The second acknowledges that economic transformation requires constitutional transformation, but a just constitutional transformation also requires economic transformation. And the third submits that Māori perspectives can help inform future economies.

Boundary struggles (stabilisation versus prefiguration)

We need to be clear: although we have taken the position that it was the expansion of capitalism from

Britain that drove colonial-capitalism in Aotearoa, this involved much more than just the dispossession of land and resources. The wounds extend across time, space, identity and minds. A narrow economic lens will never be enough to capture these. We argue that decolonisation is a necessary step towards repairing the original wounds that colonial-capitalism inflicted. Reconstructing Indigenous identity is a crucial part of this struggle, although not one we address here. We say that reconstructing identity is a key part of reconstructing culture as a mode of life. Identity will always be threatened without the material resources to build lifeways beyond colonial-capitalism.

Glen Coulthard talks about the 'liberal politics of recognition', where particular aspects of Indigenous culture are *allowed* by the capitalist state – but these do not include aspects of culture that challenge capitalist accumulation or state sovereignty.[1] In the liberal politics of recognition, cultural expressions of identity are often placed above political and economic considerations. We, however, follow Coulthard, and argue that while reconstructing identity and cultural resurgence are crucial initiatives, they are also a means of achieving the political and economic end of reconstructing lifeways. For us, decolonisation is about dismantling unjust colonial structures and rebuilding just Indigenous ones encompassing land, resources and self-determining authority. It is not only about thinking differently but also about challenging and changing the material relations of colonial-capitalism. To paraphrase Tā Tipene O'Regan, mana whenua need mana and whenua.

Some critics have argued that particular forms of rangatiratanga are capitalist and therefore should not be supported as part of economic transformation. There is a huge amount of scholarly work dissecting the ways that capitalism and colonialism intersect. While there is not enough space here to do this body of work justice, we reject claims that Māori economic strategies are valid only insofar as they are anti-capitalist. Many Māori individuals and organisations have engaged and advanced self-determination and wellbeing through capitalist relations, and we cannot diminish these efforts and outcomes despite their not necessarily aligning with our particular position. An anti-capitalist movement premised on the ongoing attempted domination of Māori is not an anti-capitalist movement worth having. Making support for Māori self-determination conditional on a set of requirements is simply more colonisation. Further, even a cursory knowledge of historical developments suggests it is impossible to build material power and achieve visions of radically different worlds without ongoing negotiation of interests and political priorities. The compromises struck to achieve the welfare state of the post-war era highlight this.

While it is true that these ideas from Māori economies present possible alternatives, it is also true that they currently help stabilise the capitalist economy. Activities like mahinga kai, unpaid labour on the marae, care labour and the services that various Māori organisations provide subsidise capitalism's ongoing operations. Capitalism requires these relations and practices to go on being unrecognised and unvalued formally to be able to maximise profits. Moreover, the ongoing existence of Māori non-capitalist relations is integral to the reproduction of capitalism. That is, the care for nature implicit in Māori economies is one way to externalise the cost of reproducing the lifeways that capital relies on.[2] It costs Māori, but it does not cost capital. Kinship relations and solidarity therefore enable Māori organisations to do well in capitalism at the same time as they maintain alternative economic possibilities. It is for this reason that our key argument is that Māori economies sit at the boundary of stabilisation and prefiguration, and are thus fundamentally important spaces for thinking strategically about a better future.

To explore this stabilisation versus prefiguration dynamic, we described the distinction between a post-settlement governance entity (PSGE) – Te Rūnanga Group – and the Māori economies of Ngāi Tahu. PSGEs have been designed to inhabit capitalism, forced into a model to achieve efficiency and navigate the imperatives of the market. We then outlined the constraints faced in resurgent Māori economies like pounamu and tītī by reviewing existing research from or associated with the Ngāi Tahu Research Centre. Despite maintaining rights and resource management practices, these practices are still constrained by waged labour, market exchange and competitive forces, both internal and external. Examples such as these have demonstrated the stabilisation–prefiguration dynamic, where the expanding but never totally dominant reach of capitalism means these economies exist on the peripheries. Continuing to exist on the peripheries is not a long-term option.

The tensions between the self-determination of Māori as tangata whenua and the operations of tangata tiriti within the web of capital have often been discussed as cultural divisions. This is in contrast to foundational divisions between systems of production, that meet on common territories, but are defined by entirely different orientations towards the relationship between humans and the rest of nature. This book raises the challenge of whether Māori-led capital accumulation and distribution activities can ever offset the 'ills' associated with stabilising colonial-capitalism, or whether they can build alternatives beyond it.

We described Te Rūnanga Group as a state-like form that is working within colonial-capitalism to advance the wellbeing of Ngāi Tahu people, while at the same time reconstructing the conditions for alternatives beyond. Te Rūnanga Group has worked through the Crown-as-capitalist state to secure a material base and to use that to advance rangatiratanga as an assertion of sovereignty. In doing so, it is maintaining and advancing the possibility of creating a new social form as part of broader struggles for constitutional transformation. This is not to erase the possibilities of other strategies for self-determination, nor to obscure the challenges of this one. While we have sympathy for critiques of Te Rūnanga Group and PSGEs, some of these critiques undermine both the pragmatic strategic potential of advancing wellbeing within the status quo and the more radical strategic possibilities of building alternatives beyond it.

As long as Te Rūnanga Group continues to be recognised as a repository of the collective rangatiratanga of

Ngāi Tahu and constituent whānau, hapū and kāinga, it has a more legitimate claim as a state-like form advancing alternative social relations than the capitalist state, whose legitimacy is weakened by the Crown's violations of Te Tiriti. But just as capital, workers and others strategically navigate the capitalist state to advance their interests, whānau, hapū and kāinga will strategically navigate Te Rūnanga Group. However, it is authority from rangatiratanga that makes Te Rūnanga Group a site for alternative possibilities. It was designed to operate within capitalism and uses extra-economic power to stabilise colonial-capitalism, but it still holds on to rangatiratanga and pre-existing social forms from Māori economies. These pre-existing social forms are directing its extra-economic powers within capitalism. While not necessarily 'revolutionary' on the surface, because not yet an outright assertion of sovereignty, the *possibilities* remain because of rangatiratanga. These can be used to prefigure other forms and challenge the assumed sovereignty of the kāwanatanga sphere to destabilise colonial-capitalist power. PSGEs and other Māori organisations can stabilise capitalism, or prefigure alternatives. It is for this reason that the assertion of sovereignty by the capitalist state is effectively a confidence trick, and for the same reason we are seeing growing racist backlash against Te Tiriti rights and co-governance. Those in power are seeing their assumption of sovereignty for capitalist accumulation challenged.

We have to reckon with power, material power. How do we transform the colonial-capitalist economy from within while transforming Māori economies? To change the economy we have to change the capitalist state. We must therefore imagine a different state, and this is where tangata tiriti who support decolonisation can focus their efforts: on transformation within the kāwanatanga sphere. The kāwanatanga sphere maintains colonial-capitalism and needs to be strategically worked through to open space for rangatiratanga and a relational sphere. This requires a state that takes kāwanatanga, rangatiratanga and the relationship between these two seriously. A future state form concerned with coordinating production and distribution of surplus would be an agglomeration of autonomous networks. It would be represented within both rangatiratanga and kāwanatanga spheres (think environmental movements, co-ops, worker collectives), strengthened, and organised into some sort of perpetually negotiable hierarchy.[3]

So what might a possible pathway look like? We, like many others, believe that constitutional transformation is fundamental to Aotearoa's future. But as we have already stated, economic transformation requires constitutional transformation, and a just constitutional transformation requires economic transformation.

Constitutional and economic transformation

From our vantage point, all signs point to inevitable constitutional transformation, and there are manifestations of this at local levels and in plain sight, driven by Māori and non-Māori committed to just futures together. The recent publications *Matike Mai* and *He Puapua* consider the ways the Crown can be held accountable for its Tiriti and other obligations in hopes of addressing the loss of rights, resources and self-determining authority through colonisation.[4] Since the publication of *Matike Mai*, which explores models for constitutional transformation, the 'spheres of influence' model has emerged in many aspects of Māori, social movement and academic thought and in public-sector consciousness. *He Puapua* builds on the insights of *Matike Mai* with a specific focus on implementation of UNDRIP, which was committed to by the National-led government in 2010. At their heart, these publications are about a just constitutional transformation.

Rangatiratanga was re-affirmed in the Ngāi Tahu Claims Settlement Act 1998. Although it is not necessarily associated with *Matike Mai* and *He Puapua* directly, there is a transformation occurring in the Ngāi Tahu region; in fact there are several transformations happening, ranging from co-governance initiatives to assertions of rangatiratanga. For example, a new entity is being formed to 'co-govern' the Ōtākaro Avon River Corridor with equal representation from Ngāi Tūāhuriri and the Christchurch City Council.[5] Former Christchurch mayor, Lianne Dalziel, says that this co-governance approach ensures the common benefit, use and enjoyment of Ngāi Tūāhuriri, Christchurch citizens and the wider community. Te Maire Tau says priorities for the land are coping with climate change, addressing water issues and encouraging feelings of community ownership. This demonstrates how mana whenua can embed long-term thinking in the use and planning of community and public land. While these initiatives all have their limits, they represent strategic navigation of existing capitalist forms.[6]

These are all examples of challenges and possible solutions for the relationship between the rangatiratanga and kāwanatanga spheres where they intersect in the relational sphere. Recently, Te Maire Tau outlined his position on rangatiratanga for Ngāi Tahu, which included title, fiscal authority and regulatory authority. This position raises several questions for us. How can Māori exercise rangatiratanga if the Crown's false assertion of sovereignty still underlies all land rights? How can Māori exercise rangatiratanga if the Crown's false assertion of sovereignty still underlies its claim to taxation, rates, levies and other forms of revenue generation? And how can Māori exercise rangatiratanga if they can't pass their own legislation to protect what they deem to be important? This necessitates a constitutional transformation that takes economic transformation seriously and allows for the economic possibilities of decolonisation.

We have to think through the economic implications and opportunities of constitutional transformation very carefully. We find ourselves in a unique version of the classic dilemma, where the capitalist state is subordinated to accumulation because it must generate revenue (e.g. taxation) to maintain itself. How does this play out when we are building the capacity for an alternative sovereignty through the state's powers? We are exacerbating the contradiction. But as it stands, the kāwanatanga sphere has powers to generate revenue through many avenues to support governance based on a false assertion of sovereignty. The rangatiratanga sphere relies on what land and resources remain, the meagre reparations of Treaty settlements and what the kāwanatanga sphere is willing to provide for Māori to exercise their obligations. This provision of funding is determined within three-year electoral cycles, and a constant rotation of public servants at central and local government levels. Resourcing rangatiratanga through the benevolence of the Crown, or the capitalist state, is hardly a long-term option. One sphere is significantly more resourced than the other, creating material power implications for the relational sphere. There is a great deal of work to be done within the kāwanatanga sphere to transform the political economy and make way for a just constitutional transformation of Aotearoa.[7]

Another lever that we and many others think is worth exploring concerns the economic implications of the guarantees in Article Two of Te Tiriti. This guarantees tino rangatiratanga over whenua, kāinga and taonga. We have established that whenua, kāinga and taonga embody all of and much more than land, villages and resources. This suggests to us that Māori lifeways are guaranteed under Te Tiriti. In particular, kāinga are intense sites of the reproduction of Māori lives that include what is commonly understood as 'the economy' but is so much more. The ability for Māori to self-determine production and reproduction must be maintained if Te Tiriti is ever to be honoured, and it is this that holds significant possibilities for economic transformation. Paul Tapsell concludes that kāinga can steer Aotearoa through troubled waters towards an inclusive economy built on partnership and equality.[8] We agree with this, but at the moment the ability of kāinga to do so is being appropriated to stabilise colonial-capitalism. For kāinga to steer towards the future, again we need to reckon with material power. While historical and existing failures through current structures suggest economic transformation including or led by Māori is necessary, Te Tiriti also demands it.

Reading the original economic instructions today

In our exploration of Māori economies in Chapter Two, we drew attention to a number of key themes that illuminate possible economic futures. These are possibilities, not set-in-stone rules advocating a blanket return to the 1700s. We explored obligations between people that established the socio-cultural relations through which Māori economies occurred. Reciprocal obligations tied people together to achieve lifeways within environmental limits. An individual within a hapū was obliged to meet economic responsibilities because of social relationships that were difficult to undermine. There was, and is, an obligation to care for the collective, overriding any right to endlessly accumulate. But exploring pre-colonial relations abstracted from current economic realities suggests only seeds of possibility. These seeds of possibility are enabled by the transformations we refer to above.

Like the removal of historically specific obligations during the transition from feudalism to capitalism, the severing of obligations between tangata and whenua in Māori economies eventually resulted in a situation where, *in general*, people demanded rights from a central capitalist state without discharging obligations to one another and nature. Despite this systemic change, these reciprocal obligations have endured in pockets of Māori society, especially at the kāinga and whānau levels. Restoring these obligations, scaling them up and out, and establishing the authority to properly exercise them beyond the capital relation could be a path towards more socially and environmentally just relations.

Taonga

Paul Tapsell stresses the importance of balance: tangata need to be in balance with whenua, to balance mauri through the equation kāinga = tangata + whenua + taonga.[9] People, land and resources were bound together by whakapapa, and this carried significant obligations. Taonga created relationships between people in a place. Resources were relations. The concept of taonga was and still is fundamental to resource management practices, and therefore to exchange, distribution and labour relations. This is especially so for mahinga kai. Although these regulations emerge from obligations to nature and ancestors, they manifest in sanctions enforced by authority and public opinion. Take rāhui (ritual prohibitions), for example: in the past, the consequences for breaching a rāhui were severe.[10] Now such possibilities are easily ignored, and the consequences for anyone enforcing a rāhui today are likely to be more severe than for those breaching it. This has implications for mauri and mana, and thus for conservation, resource stocks, and health and safety. There have been calls for greater legal recognition of rāhui.[11]

Within colonial-capitalism most of 'nature' is systematically rendered as valueless: a free or cheap resource to be consumed in production (source), or destroyed as an externality of production (sink). Exceptions to the rule of the profit imperative tend to be asserted via conservation or protection of particular sites. These exceptions generally lock in capitalist influences more broadly by holding up the extractivism of colonial-capitalism as the only way humans can engage with the rest of nature. From a Māori perspective, this is wrong. Whenua and taonga are not free or cheap. They are relations, with reciprocal obligations related to use that are carefully regulated by tohunga, rangatira and public opinion in the service of balancing mauri. Thinking more carefully through the use-value of taonga, resisting their reduction to exchange-value as commodities on the market suggests possibilities for how we use or do not use resources. This is already happening.[12]

Tauutuutu

In Māori economies, exchange practices continue the commitment to balance, embedded within the socio-cultural relations that reciprocal obligations and rights establish. Escalating reciprocal exchanges create and maintain social obligations and dynamic balance, determined and regulated by mana and mauri, and conducted within a web of whakapapa. In the past, Māori often engaged in exchange practices like tauutuutu to enhance their livelihoods, rather than to meet the basic needs of life. In this way, the practices were opportunities for exchange, not imperatives to survive.

Likewise, when Māori first came into contact with the international economy, they engaged with it on their terms to enhance their lives. This period is significant, because it was when mana and mauri were still determinative, and Māori still held sovereignty. Although Māori exchange practices have endured, they are now insufficient for Māori to meet all the needs of life. To do so today we have to engage in markets – labour markets, housing markets, rental markets, education markets and food markets. This inability to operate beyond capitalist imperatives is the distinction between the *opportunities* of non-market exchange practices and the *imperatives* of capitalism. The idea of 'mana-enhancing' or other social equivalents have been co-opted into market exchanges because capitalism develops through pre-existing forms – 'you scratch my back, I'll scratch yours'. But these market exchanges are determined by profit, not by the webs of determining relations, created by whakapapa and regulated by tikanga.

This raises the opportunity to think carefully about who we are exchanging with, and why. How can we set up direct exchange relationships that are mutually beneficial and long term, and that establish or enhance our obligations to one another and nature? We have to do this consciously, and create opportunities for an engagement with nature where mana and mauri, rather than profit, are determinative. For example, Merata Kawharu shows that a kin community micro-economy value chain can manifest with a strong community desire to connect lands and resources with descendant consumers wherever they might live.[13] Kāinga and other organisational forms might consider how they can exchange with others prior to entering the capitalist market. If, for example, kai is grown or collected at marae, decision-makers could consider layers of obligation prior to selling on the market: that is, obligations to kaumātua, whānau in need, urban descendants, and so on, all of whom can reciprocate in a multitude of ways. This requires a collective and conscious allocation of resources, planned according to need rather than profit. It is not set and forget, but creating a new determination to reproduce ourselves together.

Tikanga of distribution

Distribution is tied in with mana, where mana is attained by how much passes through one's hands rather than how much accumulates in one's hands. And, once again, distribution occurs within the relationships established by reciprocal obligations and rights. In this case, it is the delegated executive authority of persons of rank, held in check by public opinion. It is the mana of this delegated executive authority that was undermined and severed over time, and replaced by the assumed sovereignty of the capitalist state. The moment of appropriation in capitalism is structured into the capitalist state by way of contractual rights and private property, for example, but Māori economies were, and to an extent still are, driven by the accumulation of mana, which is intrinsically reciprocal. One accumulated mana through the distribution and exchange of surplus goods. Thinking about contemporary distribution practices as being about how much passes through the executive authority rather than how much is accumulated provides alternative possibilities for enhancing lifeways.

An incendiary example is that despite Aotearoa being a relatively important food producer in the global market, there is widespread food insecurity; high food prices are a central feature of a 'cost of living crisis'; and many alternative sources of food as taonga have been destroyed in pursuit of food as a commodity for export and profit. Market imperatives lead to false scarcity. Distributional obligations prevented this from happening within Māori communities, despite actual food scarcity occurring as a result of seasonality. However, there were distinctions based on the relationship to the means of production and reproduction, and executive authority over rights and resources, exchange and distribution of the surplus from these rights and resources were governed by socio-cultural relations. Socio-cultural relations, rather than the overriding profit imperative, directly influenced decisions over production and distribution of resources. This led to planned producing, exchanging and distributing for need and for the accumulation of mana. As we confront the social and ecological crises of today, planning for production, exchange and distribution becomes necessary. In what form and at what level this planning occurs remains an open question.

Hau of work

How a society organises labour is a strong measure of the capacity for a society to thrive. In Chapter Two we showed that traditionally, the fruits of Māori work were not alienated. Māori did not sell their time to someone else who owned the means of production so as to receive some portion of the value generated in that work through a wage. The introduction of wage-labour was a huge change for Māori labour relations. Critics of the Māori work ethic have failed to recognise that alienation in the wage-labour relation is discouraging. Waged labour is severed from aspirations, collective organisation, and the mana of rangatiratanga and tohunga, tapu and whakapapa. Why would Māori give all the value of their dignified labour to someone else to profit off?

Mānuka Hēnare argues that in the capitalist model workers are forced to accept fluctuating compensation irrespective of collective needs. In contrast, Māori labour incorporates the notions of tapu, mauri and mana. Māori philosophy gives dignity (tapu and mana) to people (labour). Labourers are not instruments or objects in the production process, with the value of their labour measured by the wage-relation, but are enfolded in lifeways. Hēnare concludes that hau (the vitality of a person, place or object) could be a contribution of Polynesian thought and practice towards healthy labour relations. This is in contrast to the wage relation. On the surface the wage relation can appear to have some formal equivalence, but it obscures both inequalities in labour and the fact a few who own appropriate value from those who labour.

Thinking through alternatives to the wage-labour relation in the contemporary context is difficult but urgent. Māori are by no means the only communities struggling under and against exploitative labour conditions. The erosion of worker rights, escalating precarity, stagnating wages relative to profits and the cost of living, and modern slavery affect multitudes of people. Our suggested possibilities are hardly radical given these radically bad realities. So what are the opportunities for Māori labour and appropriation of value today? For example, tūao (like working bees) are being revived as a way to reconnect. Kāinga and urban descendants return to the land, labour together, and develop a strong sense of solidarity with one another and the land, all the while re-establishing the mana of kāinga and marae, and reconnecting tangata and whenua.[14] As we have suggested, these sorts of non-waged labour can work to maintain capitalist relations when wages are still dominant, but the profound sense of value and values that manifest as part of reconnecting with one another and the land through labour needs to be thought through carefully and scaled up or out.

Finishing with more questions

This book has raised many more questions than it has answered. Our intention has been to add ideas and possibilities to an ongoing critical conversation rather than suggest that we have definitive solutions. Solutions cannot manifest exclusively in universities and books; they are manifested by people in the world together. Our intention in this book has been to bring together existing perspectives and actions as part of a conversation about a much broader and longer project. Bearing this in mind, we hope that readers, among many others, will be active contributors to these discussions. We believe more attention needs to be paid to the economic possibilities of decolonisation, and thus the economic implications of colonisation. Today the world is in the middle of a global social and ecological crisis, and because profit is dominant, despite us being conscious of what is happening, we are not taking decisive action to stop or reverse this.

In the process of writing, other issues came into view. For example, when Māori were engaging in international trade relationships prior to Te Tiriti, at what point did the social relations change from being Māori to being capitalist? It is a question that takes the distinction between commercial opportunities and market imperatives seriously.

It is also evident that significant quantities of Māori rights and resources, exchange, distribution and labour operate outside of respective markets. Immeasurable labour time goes into maintaining marae, mahinga kai, building community, and protecting and advancing rights, that is not recognised by wages or as a labour market.[15] This labour is disproportionately performed by Māori women. Should we recognise this labour through wages? This is a central debate in feminist political economy. To echo Marilyn Waring, while Māori, women's and Māori women's labour have all been historically excluded from formal recognition in 'the economy', it may well be Māori, women and Māori women whose work leads us all towards alternative futures. Waring has asked 'what if women counted?' We support and extend this by asking 'what if Māori, and especially Māori women, counted?' and, vitally, 'what if we counted in Māori?'[16]

Likewise, many taonga continue to exist outside of pricing mechanisms or asset markets. Should this continue? And gifting, koha, kai and other forms of exchanging goods and services do not involve money or money markets. Should they? These are complex questions that communities are confronting right now. Personally, we think these should be maintained and scaled up and out as alternatives, but we do not wish to prevent others from saying and trying the opposite. These sites hold so many possibilities for transformation. It is about illuminating them as alternatives to illustrate how essential they are to lifeways as part of a broader strategy for building collective power. Yes, they stabilise in some ways; yes, they can prefigure alternatives in others.

On another front, we can evaluate the strategic implications of PSGEs. Ngāi Tahu Property and other PSGE entities have turned a lot of land into assets to be exchanged on the market. The capital from these exchanges has been transformed into a passive beneficiary distribution, some of which has been given to marae to reconstruct the mana of the marae. As the marae grow as a space within and against capitalism, they demand more authority from the PSGEs. Will PSGEs and iwi as state forms wither away?

This is closely related to another pressing though not uncontroversial question. Can the money from Treaty settlements, within colonial-capitalism, be used to build structures and opportunities against and beyond it? This is a question about strategy derived from the stabilisation versus prefiguration dynamic we have highlighted – what do we do next? We are not arguing that the only route to a more just future is via capitalism, but we are here now so what do we do? Some of the hapū and whānau that have not yet gone through the Treaty settlements process, or those that have been part of transforming it, will have some answers to this as well.

What might Aotearoa's economy look like today if Te Tiriti was honoured?

It is difficult to imagine what Māori economies might look like today under different scenarios, but it is important to do so. It is key to imagining the economic possibilities of decolonisation, because Māori economies hold the seeds for prefiguring alternatives. Maybe things would have turned out the same? We doubt this. Once again, it is fascinating to think about the period between contact and Te Tiriti in terms of possible economic trajectories. The work of Hazel Petrie is illustrative here, and there is and will be more work in this realm. As Michael Stevens has said, we can use this period to prepare for the next economic transition: 'The world of our tipuna got big – really big – really quickly, but they filled that bigger space. They lived in the whole world, and we owe it to them to recommit ourselves to that horizon or vision.'[17]

Of particular interest to us is Aotearoa's relationship with the Pacific. Paul Tapsell retold Cook's arrival in *Kāinga* by asking us to imagine Tūpaea's arrival aboard the *Endeavour* from the vantage point of Māori at that time. There is a tohunga aboard the ship, expert in celestial interpretation and with knowledge of the time Māori ancestors disappeared over the horizon; he has shared ancestry with the people in this new land, and relays news of the homeland. He is gifted taonga to symbolise the importance of reunion, and he gifts his name to a chosen child. 'The name becomes your kāinga/marae community's legacy, to be passed on through the generations, marking the moment when Māori reunited with their Pacific relations.'[18]

Exploring how economic structures have endured and adapted in the Pacific and what this might mean for economic futures in Aotearoa presents a vital opportunity, similar to that of Tūpaea's reconnection. This includes the economic and social relations that have emerged as tools to retain customary land from dispossession, and alternative relations around labour and the distribution of surplus. Aotearoa is a semi-peripheral, agrarian outpost of the imperial core. This better aligns us and our economic interests with other Pacific economies, but we also think Māori economies and assertions of rangatiratanga could be informed by the lifeways of Pacific relations.[19] We encourage, and are actively part of, the sharing of knowledge and economic strategies between Māori and the Pacific, including Māori and Pacific peoples in Aotearoa. The more of this, the merrier.[20] Sharing of this kind may well provide some ideas about what Māori economies would have looked like today if Te Tiriti had been honoured, and how all peoples can be part of these economies into the future.

What are the economic opportunities and implications of constitutional transformation?

We believe this to be the most crucial question that needs to be addressed seriously, and urgently, by a lot of people.[21] And people are doing this – but there is so much work to be done to imagine and then implement an economically just constitutional transformation. First we can take a strategic relational approach.[22] What are the parts of the Crown-as-capitalist state that need to be worked on for this economically just constitutional transformation? What do we keep? What do we toss out? And what do we transform? For example, PSGEs are often identified as vehicles for self-determination, but in some ways they are also re-articulations of the Crown or, in a more generous interpretation, entities created by the Crown as new partners for itself.[23] PSGEs can advance self-determination in some ways and constrain it in others by either replacing existing social relations or obscuring them.

In addition, we have touched on the disparity in opportunities to resource rangatiratanga. Co-governance is one thing, but already the rangatiratanga sphere is much less well resourced than the kāwanatanga sphere in those relational frameworks. This raises two possibilities: one is progressing the status quo and the other is altering it. First, what are the opportunities to divert Crown funding to better resource rangatiratanga so that Māori can engage with the Crown in all aspects of governance on more equal terms? Second, what are the opportunities for Māori to directly resource their own rangatiratanga, beyond having an asset base in the colonial-capitalist economy? Is there a future in which Māori can collect taxes, rates, levies or their equivalents directly, rather than having to apply for funding from their Treaty partner? Taxation is a key basis of modern sovereignty, and Māori never ceded sovereignty. These two points get to our central tension. Are we to expect the Crown-as-capitalist state to continue to fund its own withering away? Or are we advocating for alternative approaches to sovereignty that require land back? All of this cannot be left to the market or the whims of three-year political cycles and an ever-changing stream of public servants. It must be planned based on need. And that planning for need requires coalitions committed to socially and ecologically just transformation.

We started this book with our key arguments and the concepts required to unpack them. We then set out some of the features of Māori economies prior to colonialism. The trajectory of these economies developing into colonial-capitalism was not inevitable, and Māori economies could have taken a very different path on their own terms, if particular historical events and forces had not occurred. We then explored how colonialism began to impose a capitalist system and what this meant for Māori economies. Despite Māori taking up the opportunities presented by international trade, over time these opportunities evolved into imperatives in order to meet the basic needs of life. This evolution was not inevitable but was the result of the imposition of extra-economic power expanding out from British colonial-capitalism as a temporary fix for all its ills. This extra-economic power manifested in the settler-colonial government of New Zealand, which proceeded to erase and replace Māori economies with colonial-capitalism. This erasure and replacement was never and will never be total, and today diverse systems of production and reproduction co-exist in Aotearoa, albeit with frictions between them. This co-existence, and these boundary struggles between Māori economies and lifeways and the colonial-capitalist economy, present possibilities for just economic futures for all.

Notes

Introduction

1 Although Ranginui Walker doesn't use this exact wording, he makes this broad argument by drawing attention to Māori struggles for justice. Ranginui Walker, *Ka Whawhai Tonu Matou: Struggle Without End,* (rev. edn), Penguin, Auckland, 1990. Some may take exception to our use of decolonisation because it means a lot of different things to different people. In some cases, it evokes nationalist movements of decolonisation that are about ejecting colonial authorities and peoples. Instead, we draw inspiration from materialist theories of decolonisation that have emerged from settler-colonial contexts, promoting just relationships between peoples that prioritise local autonomy and power-sharing.

2 This is the first thing that economic geographer Nicholas Lewis said to Matthew Scobie when they first met in the UK around 2018. It in part inspired this book.

3 Matike Mai was established at a meeting of the Iwi Chairs' Forum in 2010. The Independent Working Group engaged with Māori nationwide at iwi, hapū and whānau levels by facilitating 252 hui between 2012 and 2015. The terms of reference for the Working Group were: "To develop and implement a model for an inclusive Constitution for Aotearoa based on tikanga and kawa, He Whakaputanga o te Rangatiratanga o Niu Tireni of 1835, Te Tiriti o Waitangi of 1840, and other indigenous human rights instruments which enjoy a wide degree of international recognition". The Independent Working Group, Matike Mai Aotearoa, 2016, HYPERLINK "https://nwo.org.nz/wp-%20 content/uploads/2018/06/MatikeMaiAotearoa25Jan16.pdf"https://nwo.org.nz/wp- content/uploads/2018/06/MatikeMaiAotearoa25Jan16.pdf, p.7

4 O.N. Ince, *Colonial Capitalism and the Dilemmas of Liberalism,* Oxford University Press, Oxford, 2018.

5 These points have been made across political and theoretical perspectives. D. Harvey, *The New Imperialism,* Oxford University Press, Oxford, 2003; R. Luxemburg, *The Accumulation of Capital,* (2013), Routledge, New York, 1951; E.G. Wakefield, *A View of the Art of Colonization* (1849), Oxford University Press, Oxford,

1914; E. M. Wood, *The Origin of Capitalism: A Longer View*, Verso, London, 2002.

6 Wood, *The Origin of Capitalism*.

7 There are some important exceptions to this, including Brian Easton's recent work, Reserve Bank of New Zealand positioning, and the Treasury's He Ara Waiora framework. See, for example, B. Easton, *Not in Narrow Seas: The Economic History of Aotearoa New Zealand*, Victoria University Press, Wellington, 2021.

1. Theoretical Framework

1 A neoclassical economics approach is incapable of grappling with colonialism because it universalises and naturalises capitalist relations by analysing production separately from the social relations that underlie it. In this case, as we will demonstrate throughout the book, significant political power was required to bring the capitalist economy into existence and to keep it going. It is not a universal, natural or inevitable form. E. M. Wood, *Democracy Against Capitalism: Renewing Historical Materialism*, Verso, London, 2007.

2 For the sake of a general readership, this condensed version covers select, key assertions and debates that have taken up entire disciplines and libraries. We acknowledge that many crucial details are omitted. Our aim in presenting these ideas in such reduced form is to help orient readers with historical materialism generally, rather than provide a full critical account of capitalism. Classical political economy is most commonly associated with the work of David Ricardo and Adam Smith; the critique of political economy begins with the work of Karl Marx and Friedrich Engels.

3 Historical materialism also challenges the idea, which is commonly associated with the contemporary liberal left, that pure 'human greed' is the driving force of capitalism and therefore that simply curbing this 'human' impulse could halt the crisis tendencies of capitalism.

4 Wood, *Democracy Against Capitalism*, p.26.

5 This is where post-structuralists depart from our approach, a fundamental disagreement being the 'totalising' nature of capitalism (see Gibson-Graham, Cameron and Healy, 2013 and Campbell, 2020 for thoughtful post-structural analysis of economic possibilities). While we have sympathy towards the characterisation of some Marxist thought as totalising, the pendulum can swing too far the other way and miss or obscure some of the key sites of domination within capitalism, and in particular the capitalist dynamics behind primitive

accumulation and colonial-capitalism. Instead we frame capitalism as ever-expanding but never total, identifying some hope at the peripheries. This is the key to the 'stabilisation-prefiguration dynamic' that we discuss through this book. J. K. Gibson-Graham, J. Cameron, and S. Healy, *Take Back the Economy: An Ethical Guide for Transforming Our Communities.* University of Minnesota Press, Minneapolis, 2013; H. Campbell, *Farming Inside Invisible Worlds: Modernist Agriculture and its Consequences,* Bloomsbury Academic, London, 2020.

6 Wood, *Democracy Against Capitalism.*

7 The key arguments here have been the subject of entire fields of work (e.g. the Brenner debates). For our purposes (and with apologies) we may boil them down to the following opposing positions: capitalism was inevitable, and it simply took the right historical conditions for it to burst free from prior restraints and spread across the world (this takes either the orthodox political economic form or the orthodox historical materialist form); or, capitalism was the result of extremely specific historical conditions and was neither inevitable nor 'natural'. We follow the latter, which is most associated with Robert Brenner and Ellen Meiksins Wood. See R. Brenner, 'Agrarian Class Structure and Economic Development in Pre-industrial Europe', *Past & Present,* 10, 1 (1976), pp.30–75. E. M. Wood, *The Origin of Capitalism: A Longer View,* Verso, London, 2002.

8 The technical term for this relationship in historical materialism is 'exploitation'. We should note here that debates rage about how wage-labour has been associated with various forms of unwaged labour throughout the history of capitalism; for example, slavery has proven to be an ongoing feature of capitalist economies, providing vast supplies of 'free' labour and enabling massive capital accumulation.

9 There are different strands of thinking and slightly different nomenclature associated with each of these, that contemplate broadly the question of this kind of labour and its role in reproducing capitalist societies.

10 S. Federici, *Revolution at Point Zero: Housework, Reproduction and Feminist Struggle,* Common Notions, New York, 2012; M. Dalla Costa, 'Capitalism and Reproduction', *Capitalism, Nature, Socialism,* 7, 4 (1996), pp.111–21.

11 This pluriversal realm of labour is where many theorists have focused their hopes for future societies and economies, suggesting that it is where alternative ways of reproducing ourselves beyond the mechanisms of capitalism may be prefigured. See, for example, J.K. Gibson-Graham, J. Cameron and S. Healy, *Take Back the Economy: An Ethical Guide for*

Transforming Our Communities, University of Minnesota Press, Minneapolis, 2013.

12 P. Burkett, *Marx and Nature*, Palgrave MacMillan, London, 1999.

13 O'Connor's (1998) 'second contradiction' posits a central contradiction within capitalism alongside the 'first' contradiction of labour versus capital: the second contradiction emerges from individual capitals running down the 'conditions' of production through treating them as costless, naturally reproducing inputs to, and sinks for, production. O'Connor specifies the conditions as the external-physical (e.g. lakes, soils), general-communal (public infrastructure, including 'ephemeral' things like communication), and labour power. While the reproduction of some of the conditions of production might be unevenly capitalised (O'Connor, 1993), capital is driven by competition and the imperative to lower costs of production toward shedding the costs of repairing the degraded conditions of production, which then falls to the state or, where the state is subject to austerity, to no one. Hence, massive socio-ecological breakdown. J.R. O'Connor, (ed.), *Natural Causes: Essays in Ecological Marxism*, Guilford Press, New York, 1998; M. O'Connor, 'On the Misadventures of Capitalist Nature', *Capitalism Nature Socialism*, 4, 3 (1993), pp.7–40.

14 Ellen Mieksins Wood reminds us that the transition from feudalism to capitalism was not inevitable, but historically specific. The transformation of social property relations took place in the English countryside, with removal of the means of subsistence from direct producers. In the new agrarian relations, landlords derived rents from commercial profits of capitalist tenants, and the dispossessed became wage-labourers. This need for profits to meet rents created new economic imperatives, including the compulsions of competition, reinforcing and expanding the new social property relations of capitalism. Wood, *The Origin of Capitalism*, p.36.

15 Absolutely central to capitalism is the capitalist state: the set of social relations through which the power to uphold the dominant mode of production is exercised. It evolved from earlier forms of political, cultural, social and economic power into the apparatus we designate as the modern state. How to understand what the capitalist state is and does is one of the most contentious topics in the social sciences.

16 And this may also be achieved through the extraction of rents or assertion of power through monopoly or monopsony (a market in which there is only one buyer).

17 Delving into the details of growth theory is out of the scope of this text; however, the hard-wiring of growth into capitalism is

foundational to its self-expansion. This is understood across both critical political economy and neoclassical economics. For detail, see D. Harvey, *The Limits to Capital*, Basil Blackwell, Oxford, 1982; Wood, *Democracy Against Capitalism*; M. Mellor, *Feminism & Ecology*, Polity Press, London, and New York University Press, New York, 1997.

18 James O'Connor argues that periodic crises provide the opportunities for the costs of reproduction to be rationalised: O'Connor, *Natural Causes*.

19 Harvey, *The Limits to Capital*.

20 C. Comyn, *The Financial Colonisation of Aotearoa*, ESRA, Wellington, 2022.

21 We have put inverted commas around 'costs' because 'costs' mean something specific in capitalism, not just financial cost but also socio-ecological costs (externalising/externalities).

22 G. Coulthard, *Red Skin, White Masks*, University of Minnesota Press, Minneapolis, 2014; S. Barber, 'In Wakefield's Laboratory: Tangata Whenua Into Property/Labour in Te Waipounamu', *Journal of Sociology*, 56, 2 (2020), pp.229–46; A. Simpson, *Mohawk Interruptus: Political Life Across the Borders of Settler States*, Duke University Press, Durham NC, 2014; M. Wynyard, '"Not One More Bloody Acre": Land Restitution and the Treaty of Waitangi Settlement Process in Aotearoa New Zealand', *Land*, 8, 11 (2019), pp.162–76.

23 K. Marx, *Capital*, (1867), Wordsworth Editions, Ware, 2013; M. Perelman, *The Invention of Capitalism: Classical Political Economy and the Secret History of Primitive Accumulation*, Duke University Press, Durham NC, 2000.

24 Karl Marx memorably described the emergence of capitalism as 'dripping with blood '. This presentation of 'primitive accumulation' recognised that it often took extreme violence to force people away from established modes of life and into wage-labour, with all that such a world entailed. Marx, *Capital*.

25 D. Harvey, *The New Imperialism*, Oxford University Press, Oxford, 2003.

26 Some Kāi Tahu prefer the southern dialect where 'ng' becomes 'k' (among other things). But much of the modern Treaty settlement documentation uses Ng (e.g. Te Rūnanga o Ngāi Tahu). We use these interchangeably depending on the preferences of those we are citing at the time.

27 Sue Ferguson and the social reproduction theory writers are the point of reference here. C. Arruzza, T. Bhattacharya and N. Fraser, *Feminism for the 99%: A Manifesto*, Verso, London, 2019; T. Bhattacharya, 'How Not To Skip Class', in T. Bhattacharya (ed.), *Social Reproduction Theory: Remapping Class,*

Recentering Oppression, Pluto Press, London, 2017, pp.68–93; G. Di Chiro, 'Living Environmentalisms: Coalition Politics, Social Reproduction, and Environmental Justice, *Environmental Politics*, 17, 2 (2008), pp.276–98; S. Ferguson, *Women and Work: Feminism, Labour, and Social Reproduction*, Pluto Press, London, 2020.

28 R. Luxemburg, *The Accumulation of Capital*, (1913) Routledge, New York, 1951.

29 'Capitalism is a system in which command and coercion are at least as important as the relatively harmonious exchange relationships (e.g. consumer choice in competitive markets) on which the neoclassical analysis focuses.' F. Stilwell, 'Neoclassical Economics: A Long Cul-de-Sac', in G. Agyrous and F. Stilwell (eds), *Economics as a Social Science*, Pluto Press, London, 1996, p.95.

30 Coulthard, *Red Skin, White Masks*.

31 Ince, *Colonial Capitalism and the Dilemmas of Liberalism*, p.4.

32 Monopolies and extra-economic powers try to prevent this. This theory of innovation is typically associated with economist Joseph Schumpeter: see J. Schumpeter, *Capitalism, Socialism and Democracy*, Harper and Brothers, New York, 1943.

33 Luxemburg, *The Accumulation of Capital*; Wakefield, *A View of the Art of Colonization*, (1849), Oxford University Press, Oxford, 1914; Wood, *The Origin of Capitalism*.

34 Wakefield developed some of his ideas around systematic colonisation while serving time in Newgate Prison for kidnapping a fifteen-year-old heiress to secure a fortune. P. Temple, *A Sort of Conscience: The Wakefields*, Auckland University Press, Auckland, 2002.

35 Wakefield, *A View of the Art of Colonization*, p.9.

36 Ibid., p.25.

37 This follows the logic of capitalism: with workers and capital in constitutive opposition, and this dynamic reinforced by the pressures generated through competition between capitalists, class struggle determines what concessions workers are able to extract from capital. This dynamic of opposition based on material interests also exists between Indigenous peoples and the capitalist state, where rights are not given but demanded through struggle.

38 Wakefield, *A View of the Art of Colonization*, p.18.

2. Economies of Mana

1 M. Amoamo, D. Ruwhiu and L. Carter, 'Framing the Māori Economy: The Complex Business of Māori Business', *MAI*

Journal, 7, 1 (2018), pp.66–78; M. Bargh, 'Rethinking and Reshaping Indigenous Economies: Māori Geothermal Energy Enterprises', *Journal of Enterprising Communities: People and Places in the Global Economy*, 6, 20 (2012), pp.271–83.

2 M. Hēnare, 'The Economy of Mana', in D. Cooke, C. Hill, P. Baskett and R. Irwin (eds), *Beyond the Free Market: Rebuilding a Just Society in New Zealand*, Dunmore Press, Auckland, 2014, pp.65–69; M. Hēnare, 'He Whenua Rangatira: A Mana Maori History of the Early–Mid Nineteenth Century', 2021, https://cdn.auckland.ac.nz/assets/arts/schools/anthropology/rale_08_d_WEB01.pdf. See also K.M. Dell, N. Staniand and A. Nicholson, 'Economy of Mana: Where to Next?', *MAI Journal*, 7, 1 (2018), pp.51–65.

3 Another large caveat here is that we are not suggesting that these are not intimately related facets of the capitalist mode of production; however, they are commonly treated as (or take the form or appearance of being) formally distinct.

4 G. Coulthard, *Red Skin, White Masks*, University of Minnesota Press, Minneapolis, 2014.

5 While this is also true of capitalism, in Māori economies profit is not the determining force.

6 C. Meillassoux, 'From Reproduction to Production: A Marxist Approach to Economic Anthropology', *Economy and Society*, 1, 1 (1972), pp.93–105.

7 See, for example, H. Beattie and A. Anderson, *Traditional Lifeways of the Southern Māori*, Otago University Press, Dunedin, 2009; R. Firth, *Economics of the New Zealand Maori*, (2nd edn), Government Printer, Wellington, 1959. The vast majority of this chapter is drawn from Raymond Firth and where possible confirmed by contemporary Māori authors such as Hirini Moko Mead, Te Maire Tau and John Reid.

8 It would be disingenuous to view pre-colonial organisation through a rose-tinted lens. Economic position was enhanced through successful warfare, and resources were fiercely fought over (Firth, *Economics of the New Zealand Maori*; Ranginui Walker, *Ka Whawhai Tonu Matou: Struggle Without End*, (rev. edn), Penguin, Auckland, 1990. This warfare also resulted in captives of war, a phenomenon which has been equated with the institution of slavery (see H. Petrie, *Outcasts of the Gods? The Struggle Over Slavery in Maori New Zealand*, Auckland University Press, Auckland, 2015, for critical analysis). Walker argues that this institution as well as polygamy enhanced the ability of leaders to accumulate wealth and maintain position above followers (see also Firth). In some ways this is related to 'control of the means of reproduction'.

9 P. Tapsell, *Kāinga: People, Land, Belonging*, Bridget Williams Books, Wellington, 2021.

10 Ibid.

11 J. Reid and M. Rout, 'Māori Tribal Economy: Rethinking the Original Economic Institutions', 2016, https://ir.canterbury.ac.nz/handle/10092/12391 (accessed 17 October 2023); Tapsell, *Kāinga: People, Land, Belonging*.

12 An example of this is when Te Rauparaha and his forces invaded Kaiapohia and massacred its inhabitants and, in response, hapū from southern regions with muskets from sustained trade with settlers ventured north to help fight them off, and thus defend the integrity of the Ngāi Tahu iwi border. T. O'Regan, 'The Economics of Indigenous Survival', 2004 (video): https://www.youtube.com/watch?v=YXuh8jerjXg; (text): https://www.cdu.edu.au/sites/default/files/opvcil/sir-tipene-oregan-speech-2014.pdf

13 T. O'Regan, *Old Myths and New Politics: Some Contemporary Uses of Traditional History*, Bridget Williams Books, Wellington, 1991.

14 Tapsell, *Kāinga: People, Land, Belonging*. Morgan Godfery (personal communication) has also suggested that for some iwi, obligations were organised around three aspects of life: tangata, whenua and moana. Pare Hauraki in the North Island, for example, was chiefly a maritime confederation. This acknowledges the different environmental and therefore social and economic conditions around Aotearoa. Stevens argues that Māori historical and theoretical approaches are primarily focused on land, and this terrestrial bias can obscure colonial contestations of marine spaces and important instances of Māori agency and lifeways in marine settings: M.J. Stevens, 'A "Useful" Approach to Maori History', *New Zealand Journal of History*, 49, 1 (2015), pp.54–77.

15 H.M. Mead, *Tikanga Māori: Living by Māori Values*, Huia, Wellington, 2003.

16 Firth, *Economics of the New Zealand Maori*.

17 Tapsell, *Kāinga: People, Land, Belonging*.

18 J. Reid, 'Māori Land: A Strategy for Overcoming Constraints on Development', PhD thesis, Lincoln University, 2011, https://researcharchive.lincoln.ac.nz/handle/10182/4184 (accessed 17 October 2023); T. Tau, 'Property Rights in Kaiapoi', *Victoria University of Wellington Law Review*, 47 (2016), pp. 677–98; T. Tau, *Sketching a Tribal Economy: Draft Discussion Document*, University of Canterbury, Christchurch, 2016.

19 T. Tau, 'Brief of Evidence of Rawiri Te Maire Tau for Te Rūnanga o Ngāi Tahu and Ngā Rūnanga [2458/2821]', 2015, http://www.chchplan.ihp.govt.nz/wp-content/

uploads/2015/07/2458-TRoNT-Ng%C4%81-R%C5%ABnanga-Evidence-of-Te-Maire-Tau-5-11-2015.pdf

20 Reid, 'Māori Land: A Strategy for Overcoming Restraints on Development'.

21 C. Spiller, R. Maunganui Wolfgramm, E. Henry and R. Pouwhare, 'Paradigm Warriors: Advancing a Radical Ecosystems View of Collective Leadership from an Indigenous Māori Perspective', *Human Relations*, 73, 4 (2020), pp.516–43; R. Wolfgramm, C. Spiller and C. Voyageur, 'Indigenous Leadership – Editors' Introduction', *Leadership*, 12, 3 (2016), pp.263–69.

22 M. Rout, J. Reid, B. Te Aika, R. Davis and T. Tau, 'Muttonbirding: Loss of Executive Authority and Its Impact on Entrepreneurship', *Journal of Management & Organization*, 23, 6 (2017), pp.857–72.

23 A. Anderson, 'Towards an Explanation of Protohistoric Social Organisation and Settlement Patterns Amongst the Southern Ngai Tahu', *New Zealand Journal of Archaeology*, 2 (1980), pp.3–23; Rout et al., 'Muttonbirding'.

24 Scale is an important consideration, whether in the past, in present conditions or for future possibilities. These details exist for some places but are diverse across time and geography, and it is out of the scope of this book to examine them. We welcome more attention to scale.

25 Tau, *Sketching a Tribal Economy*.

26 Tau, *Sketching a Tribal Economy*; M.J. Stevens, '"A Defining Characteristic of the Southern People": Southern Māori Mobility and the Tasman World', in R. Standfield (ed.), *Indigenous Mobilities: Across and Beyond the Antipodes*, Australian National University Press, Canberra, 2018, pp.79–114.

27 J. Reid, M. Rout, J. Whitehead and Te Puoho Katene, *Tauutuutu: White Paper: Executive Summary*, Our Land and Water National Science Challenge, 2021.

28 Ibid.

29 Firth, *Economics of the New Zealand Maori*.

30 On the complexity of these social distinctions and the role of slavery, see Firth, *Economics of the New Zealand Maori* and Petrie, *Outcasts of the Gods?*.

31 Firth, *Economics of the New Zealand Maori*.

32 Ibid.

33 Ibid., pp.242–43.

34 These methods for increasing efficiency are common across labour forms, including waged labour. The difference with capitalism is that it is geared towards increasing productivity, thus surplus value (profit), and this surplus value is alienated.

3. Stabilising a Colonising Economy

1 These alternative possibilities are not solely in the realm of Māori economies but are also contained in the echoes of pre-capitalist relations still present in tangata tiriti ways of organising.
E.G. Wakefield, in *A View of the Art of Colonization*, (1849), Oxford University Press, Oxford, 1914, was clear that they couldn't just send settlers over because they would possibly just return to subsistence living, or even be subsumed into Māori economies. They had to be forced into capitalist social relations and this was a key part of systematic colonisation.

2 H. Petrie, *Chiefs of Industry: Māori Tribal Enterprise in Early Colonial New Zealand*, Auckland University Press, Auckland, 2006.

3 Ibid.

4 A. Anderson, J. Binney and A. Harris, *Tangata Whenua: An Illustrated History*, Bridget Williams Books, Wellington, 2016.

5 Ibid.; M.J. Stevens, 'A "Useful" Approach to Maori History', *New Zealand Journal of History*, 49, 1, (2015), pp.55–77.

6 Petrie, *Chiefs of Industry*.

7 P. Tapsell, *Kāinga: People, Land, Belonging*, Bridget Williams Books, Wellington, 2021.

8 A. Anderson, *A Welcome of Strangers: An Ethno-history of Southern Maori A.D. 1650–1850*, Otago University Press, Dunedin, 1998, as cited in M.J. Stevens, '"A Defining Characteristic of the Southern People": Southern Māori Mobility and the Tasman World', in R. Standfield (ed.), *Indigenous Mobilities: Across and Beyond the Antipodes*, Australian National University Press, Canberra, 2018, pp.79–114.

9 J. Belich, *Making Peoples: A History of the New Zealanders—From Polynesian Settlement to the End of the Nineteenth Century*, Penguin, Auckland, 1996; Stevens, '"A Defining Characteristic of the Southern People"'.

10 M. Stevens in L. Steyl, 'What Murihiku Learned from Past Transformations', Stuff, 10 January 2022, https://www.stuff.co.nz/pou-tiaki/127258286/what-murihiku-learned-from-past-transformations (accessed 17 October 2023).

11 K. Stevens and A. Wanhalla, 'Intimate Relations: Kinship and the Economics of Shore Whaling in Southern New Zealand, 1820–1860', *Journal of Pacific History*, 52, 2 (2017), pp.135–55; A. Wanhalla, *In/visible Sight: The Mixed-Descent Families of Southern New Zealand*, Bridget Williams Books, Wellington, 2015.

12 Stevens and Wanhalla, 'Intimate Relations'.

13 Ibid.

14 Ibid.

15 E.P. Thompson, *The Making of the English Working Class*, Vintage Books, New York, 1963; C. Comyn, *The Financial Colonisation of Aotearoa*, ESRA, Wellington, 2022; P. Mein-Smith and M.A. Wyndham, *History of Australia, New Zealand and the Pacific*, Blackwell, Oxford, 2000.

16 Thompson, *The Making of the English Working Class.*

17 Even though these are typically regressively funded through the wages of the workers themselves, rather than from the pockets of the capitalists relying on healthy labour forces.

18 For a critical approach, see D. Harvey, *The New Imperialism*, Oxford University Press, Oxford, 2003. And for a supportive approach, see Wakefield, *A View of the Art of Colonization.*

19 B. Bradby, 'The Destruction of Natural Economy', *Economy and Society*, 4, 2 (1975), p.138.

20 Catherine Comyn provides a fine-tooth-comb analysis of the relationship between the New Zealand Company and the Crown. We quote her in full: 'To purchase land in a country 25,000 kilometres away, land inhabited by another people whose "sovereignty" was affirmed by the British Colonial Office at the time, and which had not been set foot on by those offering it up for sale, would have appeared an excessively risky investment if it were not for the racist and colonialist cultural logics that had marked European consciousness for centuries. Central here is the assumption that, because Indigenous peoples' lands were not privatised and developed according to the capitalist mode of production, they were terra nullius: "land belonging to no-one". The supposed absence of Indigenous peoples' land rights – an absence actually constructed through a determined denial of Indigenous systems of land tenure – was used to legitimise Europeans in occupying, privatising, and controlling their lands and resources.' C. Comyn, ' How Finance Colonised Aotearoa: A Concise Counter-History', *Counterfutures*, 7 (2019), p.7.

21 For a couple of great texts see: Anderson, Binney and Harris, *Tangata Whenua*; C. Orange, *The Treaty of Waitangi*, Bridget Williams Books, Wellington, 1987; Ranginui Walker, *Ka Whawhai Tonu Matou: Struggle Without End*, (rev. edn), Penguin, Auckland, 1990.

22 M. Mutu, 'Behind the Smoke and Mirrors of the Treaty of Waitangi Claims Settlement Process in New Zealand: No Prospect for Justice and Reconciliation for Māori Without Constitutional Transformation', *Journal of Global Ethics*, 14, 2 (2018), pp.208–21.

23 Ned Fletcher's recent intervention broadly argues that the Treaty and Te Tiriti can be reconciled based on British understandings of sovereignty as accommodating plurality at the time of signing.

N. Fletcher, *The English Text of the Treaty of Waitangi*, Bridget Williams Books, Wellington, 2022.

24 S. Barber, 'In Wakefield's Laboratory: Tangata Whenua Into Property/Labour in Te Waipounamu', *Journal of Sociology*, 56, 2 (2020), pp.229–46; M. Wynyard, '"Not One more Bloody Acre": Land Restitution and the Treaty of Waitangi Settlement Process in Aotearoa New Zealand', *Land*, 8, 11 (2019), pp.162–76.

25 Stuff.co.nz published an interactive 'Nā Niu Tīreni: New Zealand Made', which features a useful illustration of Māori land loss over time: https://interactives.stuff.co.nz/2018/07/na-niu-tireni-new-zealand-made/ (accessed 17 October 2023).

26 Barber, 'In Wakefield's Laboratory'.

27 Waitangi Tribunal. 'The Ngāi Tahu Report (Vol 3), 1991, http://https://forms.justice.govt.nz/search/Documents/WT/wt_DOC_160762113/Ngai%20Tahu%20Report%201991%20V3W.pdf (accessed 10 January 2023), p. 1051.

28 Ibid.

29 Comyn, 'How Finance Colonised Aotearoa'.

30 Ibid., p.63.

31 This Crown backing of failed speculative endeavours is by no means a thing of the past, with the South Canterbury Finance bailout far exceeding the financial value of any particular Treaty settlement. A. Bennett, ' South Canterbury Bailout Bill: $405 Each', *New Zealand Herald*, 1 September 2020, https://www.nzherald.co.nz/business/south-canterbury-bailout-bill-405-each/7X6HE2HIBLAEA6KFKJBIY66UDE/(accessed 17 October 2023).

32 K. Hooper and K. Kearins, 'Substance But Not Form: Capital Taxation and Public Finance in New Zealand, 1840–1859', *Accounting History*, 8, 2 (2003), pp.101–19.

33 Comyn, *The Financial Colonisation of Aotearoa*. The bases upon which speculation had been occurring were not strong enough to ensure enforcement of the 'absolute private property' required for capitalist speculation. Because we think of the state as a 'material condensate of the balance of class struggle' and thus the early state (extra-economic power) as working towards becoming a capitalist state (or forces acting on and through it as working towards a capitalist state), we can see pre-emption as a mechanism by which future accumulation was secured. N.A. Poulantzas, *State, Power, Socialism*, Vol. 29, Verso, London, 1978.

34 c.f. C. Parenti, 'The 2013 ANTIPODE AAG Lecture: The Environment Making State: Territory, Nature, and Value', *Antipode*, 47, 4 (2015), pp.829–48.

35 Wakefield, *A View of the Art of Colonization*, p.19.

36 In ibid., p.55, Wakefield goes on to make some incredibly racist

remarks about Black and Irish people as part of a critique of slavery.

37 Much of this land was returned to individuals, and often the wrong ones, during compensation of the mid-1960s–70s. These lands were confiscated collectively and returned individually, and this flawed process had major long-term repercussions.

38 Petrie, *Chiefs of Industry.*

39 For example, V. O'Malley, *The New Zealand Wars| Ngā Pakanga o Aotearoa*, Bridget Williams Books, Wellington, 2019; J. Kidman, V. O'Malley, L. MacDonald, T. Roa and K. Wallis, *Fragments from a Contested Past: Remembering and Forgetting Difficult Histories*, Bridget Williams Books, Wellington, 2022; Walker, *Ka Whawhai Tonu Matou.*

40 Tapsell, *Kāinga: People, Land, Belonging.*

41 J. Belich, *Making Peoples: A History of the New Zealanders from Polynesian Settlement to the End of the Nineteenth Century*, University of Hawai'i Press: Honolulu, 1996, p.258, as cited in Wynyard, '"Not One More Bloody Acre"'.

42 'By 1912, over 200 properties, comprising 1,300,000 acres, had been purchased and subdivided [by the government]; 17,000 people were living on land which had been almost uninhabited [...] For the first time there was one system of land regulations' (Sinclair, 1988, p.179). The nature of tenure over land was a matter of great contention: in the end a 'lease in perpetuity' (999 years) with 'no provision to secure for the public purse a share in future increases in land values' was enacted (Sinclair, 1988, p.180). These small farmers were formerly working class and the transformation to petty bourgeoisie is a key piece of understanding colonial-capitalism in New Zealand. K. Sinclair, *A History of New Zealand*, (3rd edn), Penguin Books Ltd, Auckland, 1988, as cited in A. Sturman, 'Capital, the State and Climate Change in Aotearoa New Zealand', doctoral dissertation, University of Sydney, 2021.

43 Wynyard, '"Not One More Bloody Acre"'.

44 K. Hooper and K. Kearins, 'The Walrus, Carpenter and Oysters: Liberal Reform, Hypocrisy and Expertocracy in Maori Land Loss in New Zealand 1885–1911', *Critical Perspectives on Accounting*, 12 (2008), pp.1239–62.

45 Petrie, *Chiefs of Industry.*

46 T. Tau, 'Brief of evidence of Rawiri Te Maire Tau for Te Rūnanga o Ngāi Tahu and Ngā Rūnanga [2458/2821]', 2015, www.chchplan.lhp.govt.nz/wp-content/uploads/2015/07/2458-TRoNT-Ng%C4%81-R%C5%ABnanga-Evidence-of-Te-Maire-Tau-5-11-2015.pdf (accessed 17 October 2023).

47 Tapsell, *Kāinga: People, Land, Belonging.*

48 See also E.S. Poata-Smith, 'The Political Economy of Māori Protest Politics, 1968–1995: A Marxist Analysis of the Roots of Maori Oppression and the Politics of Resistance', doctoral dissertation, University of Otago, 2002.

49 Tapsell, *Kāinga: People, Land, Belonging.*

50 Stevens, 'A "Useful" Approach to Maori History'.

51 T. Tau, 'Kā Wai o Tahu: Ngāi Tahu's Legal Action Over Water', Word Festival, Christchurch, 2021, https://word2021.wordchristchurch.co.nz/programme/ka-wai-o-tahu-ngai-tahus-legal-action-over-water/ (accessed 17 October 2023).

52 Petrie, *Chiefs of Industry.*

53 M. Scobie, G. Finau and J. Hallenbeck, 'Land, Land Banks and Land Back: Accounting, Social Reproduction and Indigenous Resurgence', *Environment and Planning A: Economy and Space,* 19 November 2021.

54 Barber, 'In Wakefield's Laboratory'; Tapsell, *Kāinga: People, Land, Belonging.*

55 A. Fyers, 'The Amount Allocated to Treaty of Waitangi Settlements is Tiny, Compared with Other Government Spending', Stuff, 3 August 2018, https://www.stuff.co.nz/national/104205997/the-amount-allocated-to-treaty-settlements-is-tiny-compared-with-other-government-spending (accessed 17 October 2023).

56 Wynyard, '"Not One More Bloody Acre"'.

57 Te Rūnanga o Ngāi Tahu (TRoNT), 'Matiaha Tiramōrehu', 2017, http://Ngāitahu.iwi.nz/our_stories/matiaha-tiramorehu-the-first-formal-statement-of-Ngāi-tahu-grievances-against-the-crown/ (accessed 17 October 2023).

58 TRoNT, *'Te Whakataunga: Celebrating Te Kerēme – the Ngāi Tahu Claim',* n.d., http://Ngāitahu.iwi.nz/Ngāi-tahu/te-whakataunga-celebrating-te-kereme-the-Ngāi-tahu-claim/ (accessed 17 October 2023).

59 Ibid.

60 T. O'Regan, *Old Myths and New Politics: Some Contemporary Uses of Traditional History,* Bridget Williams Books, Wellington, 1991; T. O'Regan, 'The Economics of Indigenous Survival', 2004: (video): https://www.youtube.com/watch?v=Yxuh8jerjXg; (text): https://www.cdu.edu.au/sites/default/files/oprcil/sir-tipene-oregan-speech-2014.pdf; TRoNT, 'Te Whakataunga'.

61 M. Fisher, *A Long Time Coming: The Story of Ngāi Tahu's Treaty Settlement Negotiations with the Crown,* Canterbury University Press, Christchurch, 2020; see also TRoNT, 'Te Whakataunga'.

62 Reparations can be understood in diverse ways depending on the context, motivations and theoretical perspective. See J. Hayward, 'Treaty of Waitangi Settlements: Successful

Symbolic Reparation', in J. Luetjens, M. Mintrom and P. Hart (eds), *Successful Public Policy: Lessons from Australia and New Zealand*, 2019, Australian National University Press, Canberra, pp.399–421; D. Stone, 'Financial and Commercial Dimensions of Settlements', in N.R. Wheen and J. Hayward (eds), *Treaty of Waitangi Settlements*, Bridget Williams Books, Wellington, 2012, pp.138–48 for 'redress'; and for international perspectives pushing boundaries of reparations see O.O. Táíwò, *Reconsidering Reparations*, Oxford University Press, Oxford, 2022; T.N. Coates, The Case for Reparations', in *The Best American Magazine Writing 2015*, Columbia University Press, New York, 2015, pp.1–50.

63 T. O'Regan, 'Te Kerēme – A Reflection', 2017, http://ngaitahu.iwi.nz/our_stories/te-kereme-reflection-tk75/ (accessed 17 October 2023); T. O'Regan, 'Tipene O'Regan: We Must Remember to Remember', *e-Tangata*, 2018, https://e-tangata.co.nz/korero/tipene-oregan-we-must-remember-to-remember/ (accessed 17 October 2023).

64 The nominal $170 million quantum has a number of bolt-ons that significantly increase its financial value, including right of first refusal, a deferred selection process, payment of interest, and a relativity clause. The 'fiscal envelope' was introduced by the government in 1994; it stated that the total value of all Treaty settlements throughout the country would be NZ$1 billion. Given that Ngāi Tahu received cash and land valued at $170 million and this was calculated to be less than 1 per cent of a number of valuations of the economic loss suffered by the iwi, Ngāi Tahu, along with Waikato-Tainui, negotiated a relativity clause that said that they were entitled to 16.1 per cent (17 per cent for Tainui) of any amount that exceeded that fiscal cap in the future. The fiscal cap has since been rescinded. M. Fisher, 'Balancing Rangatiratanga and Kāwanatanga: Waikato-Tainui and Ngāi Tahu's Treaty Settlement Negotiations with the Crown', PhD thesis, Victoria University of Wellington, 2015, http://researcharchive.vuw.ac.nz/xmlui/handle/10063/4642 (accessed 17 October 2023); Fisher, *A Long Time Coming*.

65 Fisher, *A Long Time Coming*.

66 Fisher, 'Balancing Rangatiratanga and Kāwanatanga'.

67 Barber, 'In Wakefield's Laboratory'.

68 A. Mikaere, *Colonising Myths: Māori Realities*, Huia, Wellington, 2011.

69 M. Stevens, 'Te Ao Hou Realised or Te Ao Hou Redux?', panel discussion on Ngāi Tahu settlement, Queenstown, 2016.

70 Tapsell, *Kāinga: People, Land, Belonging*.

71 Mutu, 'Behind the Smoke and Mirrors of the Treaty of Waitangi

Claims Settlement Process'; M. Mutu, '"To Honour the Treaty, We Must First Settle Colonisation", (Moana Jackson 2015): The Long Road from Colonial Devastation to Balance, Peace and Harmony', *Journal of the Royal Society of New Zealand*, 49, supplement 1, (2019), pp.4–18; M. Mutu, 'The Treaty Claims Settlement Process in New Zealand and its Impact on Māori', *Land*, 8, 10 (2019), p.152.

72 In the Lands case, *New Zealand Maori Council v Attorney-General 1987*, the Court of Appeal directed the Crown to prepare safeguards to ensure that the transfer of lands was consistent with Treaty principles. The Crown reached an out-of-court agreement with the Māori Council that resulted in legislative amendments to empower the Waitangi Tribunal to order that state-owned enterprise, Crown forest and certain other lands be returned to Māori, along with compensation for forests. See Mutu, 'To Honour the Treaty, We Must First Settle Colonisation'.

73 Mutu, 'Behind the Smoke and Mirrors of the Treaty of Waitangi Claims Settlement Process', p.214.

74 M. Bargh, 'Post Settlement World (So Far): Impacts for Māori', in Wheen and Hayward (eds), *Treaty of Waitangi Settlements*, pp.166–81, as cited in Mutu, 'To Honour the Treaty, We Must First Settle Colonisation'.

75 The Independent Working Group, *Matike Mai Aotearoa*, 2016, https://www.nwo.org.nz/wp-content/uploads/2018/06/MatikeMaiAotearoa25Jan16.pdf.

76 C. Charters, K. Kingdon-Bebb, T. Olsen, W. Ormsby, E. Owen, J. Ruru, N. Solomon, G. Williams and J. Pryor, *He Puapua: Report of the Working Group on a Plan to Realise the UN Declaration on the Rights of Indigenous Peoples in Aotearoa, New Zealand*, 2019, https://iwichairs.maori.nz/wp-content/uploads/2015/07/He-Puapua-for-OIA-release.pdf; M. Godfery, 'The Political Constitution: From Westminster to Waitangi', *Political Science*, 68, 2 (2016), pp.192–209.

4. Diverse Economies in Aotearoa

1 T. O'Regan, 'The Economics of Indigenous Survival', 2004, (video): https://www.youtube.com/watch?v=YXuh8jerjXg; (text): https://www.cdu.edu.au/sites/default/files/opveil/sire-tipene-oregan-speech-2014.pdf.

2 M. Amoamo, D. Ruwhiu and L. Carter, 'Framing the Māori Economy: The Complex Business of Māori Business', *MAI Journal*, 7, 1 (2018), pp.66–78.

3 T. Tau and M. Rout, 'The Tribal Economy', *Journal of New Zealand Studies*, 27 (2018), pp.92–109. M. Scobie and A. Sturman,

'Economies of Mana and Mahi Beyond the Crisis, *New Zealand Journal of Employment Relations*, 45, 2 (2020), pp.77–88.

4 Here we are paraphrasing T. Tau, 'Kā Wai o Tahu: Ngāi Tahu's Legal Action Over Water', WORD Festival, Christchurch, 2021, https://word2021.wordchristchurch.co.nz/programme/ka-wai-o-tahu-ngai-tahus-legal-action-over-water (17 October 2023).

5 T. Tau, 'Neo-liberal Settlements: From Adam Smith to Treaty Settlements', *New Zealand Journal of History*, 49, 1 (2015), pp.126–44.

6 B. Easton, *Not in Narrow Seas: The Economic History of Aotearoa New Zealand*, Victoria University Press, Wellington, 2021; J. Kelsey, *The New Zealand Experiment: A World Model for Structural Adjustment?*, Bridget Williams Books, Wellington, 1995; J. Kelsey, *The Fire Economy: New Zealand's Reckoning*, Bridget Williams Books, Wellington, 2015.

7 Tau, 'Neo-liberal Settlements'.

8 See D. Harvey, *A Brief History of Neoliberalism*, Oxford University Press, Oxford, 2007, and B. Dunn, 'Against Neoliberalism as a Concept', *Capital & Class*, 41, 3 (2017), pp.435–54.

9 Notably, the expansive colonial state which embodied collectivised social reproduction across much of the pre-neoliberal twentieth century was the direct result of struggles between the working class, small farmers and capital that had raged from the late eighteenth century through to the Great Depression. When the compromises embodied in this expansive state were dismantled in the 1980s and '90s, communities and individuals were forced to find new ways to care for and reproduce themselves – for many, this meant the expansion of personal debt. See N. Fraser, 'Crisis of Care? On the Social-Reproductive Contradictions of Contemporary Capitalism', in T. Bhattacharya (ed.), *Social Reproduction Theory: Remapping Class, Recentring Oppression*, Pluto Press, London, 2017, pp.21–36.

10 O'Regan, 'The Economics of Indigenous Survival'.

11 The organisational structure was depicted at the Ngāi Tahu website, but no longer appears there. This depiction is accessible in M. Scobie, 'Grounding the Concept and Practice of Accountability: A Case Study with Ngāi Tahu', doctoral dissertation, University of Sheffield, 2019, p.79, https://etheses.whiterose.ac.uk/24237/ (accessed 17 October 2023).

12 TRoNT, *Te Rūnanga o Ngāi Tahu*, https://ngaitahu.iwi.nz/te-runanga-o-ngai-tahu/ (accessed 30 November 2023).

13 M. Scobie, B. Lee and S. Smyth, 'Grounded Accountability and Indigenous Self-determination', *Critical Perspectives on Accounting*, 92 (2023), pp.1–19, https://doi.org/10.1016/j.cpa.2020.102198 (accessed 17 October 2023).

14 A. Poyser, A. Scott and A. Gilbert, 'Indigenous Investments: Are They Different? Lessons from Iwi', *Australian Journal of Management*, 46, 2 (2021), pp.287–303; E. Henry and A. Poyser, 'Indigenous History, Culture and Values as Investment Philosophy: Lessons from the New Zealand Māori', *Journal of Sustainable Finance & Investment*, (2022), pp.1–13, https://doi.org/10.1080/20430795.2022.2040944 (accessed 17 October 2023).

15 S. Barber, 'In Wakefield's Laboratory: Tangata Whenua Into Property/Labour in Te Waipounamu', *Journal of Sociology*, 56, 2 (2020), pp.229–46.

16 According to the Charter of Te Rūnanga o Ngāi Tahu, Te Rūnanga has been established for a number of reasons including:

- As a repository of collective tino rangatiratanga of Ngāi Tahu Whānui.
- To represent the collective interest and be legal representative of Ngāi Tahu Whānui.
- To receive assets and assume liabilities of the former representative Ngāi Tahu Māori Trust Board and those transferred by the Crown.
- To act as Trustee of the Charitable Trust.

See also Tā Tipene O'Regan's reflections on the importance of rangatiratanga and the post settlement structure: https://ngaitahu.iwi.nz/our_stories/te-kereme-reflection-tk75/ (accessed 17 October 2023).

17 TRoNT, *2021 Annual Report*, https://ngaitahu.iwi.nz/investment/ngai-tahu-annual-reports/ (accessed 17 October 2023).

18 TRoNT, *Ngāi Tahu 2025*, 2012,https://ngaitahu.iwi.nz/te-runanga-o-ngai-tahu/our-work-pou/ngai-tahu-2/ (accessed 29 January 2024).

19 O'Regan, 'The Economics of Indigenous Survival'.

20 Ibid.

21 Te Rūnanga o Ngāi Tahu, 'Partnership to Protect and Conserve Archival Taonga Celebrated', 2021, https://ngaitahu.iwi.nz/connect-2/connect/media/partnership-to-protect-and-conserve-archival-taonga-celebrated/ (accessed 29 January 2024).

22 See, for example, TRoNT, 'Te Whakataunga: Celebrating Te Kerēme – The Ngāi Tahu Claim', n.d., http://ngaitahuiwi.nz/ngai-tahu/te-whakataunga-celebrating-te-kereme-the-ngai-tahu-claim/ (accessed 17 October 2023).

23 Kotahi Mano Kāika, 'Kotahi Mano Kāika', n.d., http://www.kmk.maori.nz/ (accessed 17 October 2023).

24 TRoNT, *2021 Annual Report*.

25 See examples of support into housing: T. Guest, 'Ngāi Tahu-

Run Scheme Opens Door to Home Ownership for Dozens of Whānau', RNZ, 5 July 2002, https://www.rnz.co.nz/news/te-manu-korihi/470370/Ngāi-tahu-run-scheme-opens-door-to-home-ownership-for-dozens-of-whanau (accessed 17 October 2023); health support: 'Covid-19 Update to Whānau', Te Rūnanga o Ngāi Tahu, 1 April 2020, https://Ngāitahu.iwi.nz/our_stories/covid-19-update-to-whanau-1-april/ (accessed 17 October 2023); and emergency response: C.M. Kenney and S. Phibbs, 'A Māori Love Story: Community-led Disaster Management in Response to the Ōtautahi (Christchurch) Earthquakes as a Framework for Action', *International Journal of Disaster Risk Reduction*, 14 (2015), pp. 46–55.

26 M. Scobie, 'The Original Instructions of Accountability: Pandemic Response as Old Ways and New Means', in S. Ratuva, Y. Crichton-Hill, T. Ross, A. Basu and P. Vakaoti (eds), *COVID-19, Social Protection and Resilience: A Comparative Approach*, Springer, Singapore, 2021.

27 O'Regan, 'The Economics of Indigenous Survival'; J. Reid and M. Rout, 'Māori Tribal Economy: Rethinking the Original Economic Institutions', 2016, https://ir.canterbury.ac.nz/handle/100092/12391 (accessed 17 October 2023); Tapsell, *Kāinga: People, Land, Belonging*, Bridget Williams Books, Wellington, 2021.

28 See, for example, 'November 2000 Contents', *Māori Law Review*, 2000, http://maorilawreview.co.nz/2000/11/november-2000-contents/

29 TRoNT, *2012 Annual Report*, https://ngaitahu.iwi.nz/investment/ngai-tahu-annual-reports/ (accessed 17 October 2023).

30 C. Charters and A. Erueti, 'Report from the Inside: The CERD Committee's Review of the Foreshore and Seabed Act 2004', *Victoria University of Wellington Law Review*, 36 (2005), pp.257–90.

31 TRoNT, 'Opening Legal Submissions on Behalf of Te Rūnanga o Ngāi Tahu and Ngā Rūnanga (Submitter #2458/Further Submission #2821)', 2015, https://chchplan.ihp.govt.nz/wp-content/uploads/2015/07/2458-TRONT-Opening-legal-submissions-22-11-2015.pdf

32 TRoNT, 'Climate Change', 2022, https://Ngāitahu.iwi.nz/environment/climate-change/ (accessed 17 October 2023).

33 This links to broader arguments of Maria Rosa Dalla Costa's critique of the expansive welfare state in the twentieth century, leading to the decimation of collectivised social reproduction. While strategically these things were good for people's livelihoods they defanged collective organising and create passive recipients of previous wins. M. Dalla Costa, *Family, Welfare and the State:*

Between Progressivism and the New Deal, Common Notions, New York, 2015.

34 T. Tau, 'Towards Tino Rangatiratanga', inaugural professorial lecture in the Law Speaker series, University of Canterbury, Christchurch, 2022.

35 M. Wynyard, '"Not One More Bloody Acre": Land Restitution and the Treaty of Waitangi Settlement Process in Aotearoa New Zealand', *Land*, 8, 11 (2019), pp.162–76.

36 A. Brankin, 'Tūrangawaewae: Where Do We Stand?', Te Karaka, 21 March 2017, http://Ngāitahu.iwi.nz/our_stories/tk73-turangawaewae-where-do-we-stand/ (accessed 17 October 2023).

37 T. O'Regan, 'Te Kerēme – A Reflection', Te Karaka.

38 A. Sturman, 'Capital, the State and Climate Change in Aotearoa New Zealand', doctoral dissertation, University of Sydney, 2021. For a detailed insider view of aspirations and challenges to do dairy better, a detailed blog can be followed at: www.happycowmilk.co.nz

39 C. Mitchell, 'I am ashamed': A Canterbury River's Pollution Starts a Cultural Debate', *Press*, 2 June 2018, https://www.stuff.co.nz/environment/104351892/i-am-ashamed-a-rivers-pollution-starts-a-cultural-debate (accessed 17 October 2023).

40 This is an example of James O'Connor's second contradiction.

41 T. Tau, 'How One Iwi is Navigating Farming While Caring for Wai Māori', Stuff, 15 June 2022, https://www.stuff.co.nz/pou-tiaki/300581544/how-one-iwi-is-navigating-farming-while-caring-for-wai-mori?utm_source=dlvr.it&utm_medium=twitter (accessed 17 October 2023).

42 M. Rout and J. Reid, 'The Historic and Contemporary Tītī and Pounamu Economies', Ngāi Tahu Research Centre, Christchurch 2019, https://www.canterbury.ac.nz/ntrc/research/ntrc-contemporary-research-division/ (accessed 17 October 2023).

43 Ibid.

44 M. Rout, J. Reid, B. Te Aika, R. Davis and T. Tau, 'Muttonbirding: Loss of Executive Authority and Its Impact on Entrepreneurship', *Journal of Management & Organization*, 23, 6 (2012), pp.857–72; A. Anderson, 'Towards an Explanation of Protohistoric Social Organisation and Settlement Patterns Amongst the Southern Ngai Tahu', *New Zealand Journal of Archaeology*, 2 (1980), pp.3–23; Rout and Reid, 'The Historic and Contemporary Tītī and Pounamu Economies'.

45 And some were not reserved. This led to a complex set-up that is detailed in Rout et al., 'Muttonbirding'.

46 For example, 'Pōhā – Ngāi Tahu Mahinga Kai', https://www.youtube.com/watch?v=IwVMlODvWNc&t=230s (accessed 17 October 2023).

47 Rout et al., 'Muttonbirding'.

48 T. Barr and J. Reid, 'Centralized Decentralization for Tribal Business Development', *Journal of Enterprising Communities: People and Places in the Global Economy*, 8, 3 (2014), pp.217–32.

49 This jade was often worked into Māori designs and passed off as authentic pounamu. This is in a similar realm to champagne and bubbly, though has additional implications because of colonialism.

50 'The raw stone is harvested and cut by Kaitiaki Rūnanga, then made available for sale on the website to carvers who are licensed to purchase raw stone. The carvers are then required to weigh, photograph and attach a unique code to every piece they carve, after which this information is uploaded onto the Ngāi Tahu Pounamu website. Through this system, the size, weight and texture of the finished items can be compared to the size, weight and texture of the original raw stone. This enables the identification of fraud, or stone laundering, and provides assurance to consumers that they are getting genuine pounamu.' Barr and Reid, 'Centralized Decentralization for Tribal Business Development', p.224.

51 This opting out occurs for a number of reasons but includes rangatiratanga and mana over whakairo (carving) and taonga, deeply important activities for many individuals and groups.

52 TRoNT, 'Haea te Awa', 2020, https://Ngāitahu.iwi.nz/runanga/haea-te-awa/ (accessed 17 October 2023).

53 Scobie, Lee and Smyth, 'Grounded Accountability and Indigenous Self-determination'.

5. Alternative Economies Are Possible

1 Glen Coulthard draws heavily from Frantz Fanon for this argument. Coulthard, *Red Skin, White Masks*, University of Minnesota Press, Minneapolis, 2014; F. Fanon, *Black Skin, White Masks*, MacGibbon & Kee, London, 1968.

2 Here we refer the reader back to the discussion of conditions of production in Chapter One, specifically the work of James O'Connor and the second contradiction of capitalism (the tendency to rapidly degrade the socio-ecological conditions of production). In a Māori context, Ellen Tapsell has explored these challenges in 'Transitioning Environmental Governance in Aotearoa: Tikanga Māori and a Political Ethic of Care', MA thesis, Victoria University of Wellington, 2022, https://openaccess.wgtn.ac.nz/articles/thesis/TRANSITIONING_ENVIRONMENTAL_GOVERNANCE_IN_AOTEAROA_TIKANGA_M_ORI_AND_A_

POLITICAL_ETHIC_OF_CARE/21685091 (accessed 17 October 2023).

3 A. Sturman, 'Capital, the State and Climate Change in Aotearoa New Zealand', doctoral dissertation, University of Sydney, 2021.

4 The Independent Working Group, *Matike Mai Aotearoa*, 2016, https://nwo.org.nz/wp-content/uploads/2018/06/MatikeMaiAotearoa25Jan2016, (accessed 17 October 2023); C. Charters, K. Kingdon-Bebb, T. Olsen, W. Ormsby, E. Owen, J. Ruru, N. Solomon, G. Williams and J. Pryor, *He Puapua: Report of the Working Group on a Plan to Realise the UN Declaration on the Rights of Indigenous Peoples in Aotearoa, New Zealand*, 2019, https://iwichairs.maori.nz/wp-content/uploads/2015/07/he-puapua-for-OIA-release.pdf (accessed 17 October 2023).

5 L. McDonald, 'City Council and Hapū Will Co-govern Christchurch's Riverside Red Zone', Stuff, 15 December 2021, https://www.stuff.co.nz/national/127263900/city-council-and-hap-will-cogovern-christchurchs-riverside-red-zone (accessed 17 October 2023).

6 An aspect of this discussion which we have paid relatively little attention to is the international context within which New Zealand's colonial-capitalist economy exists. Historically and currently, the small, extremely open and export-driven economy is a price taker, and this extends to the ecological 'costs' of, for example, industrial agriculture. Ultimately, the ability to limit ecological degradation from production will have to take into account how New Zealand will be linked to the global capitalist economy, and how any changes will be achieved there.

7 Sturman, 'Capital, the State and Climate Change in Aotearoa New Zealand'; M. Scobie, A. Heyes, R. Evans and P. Fukofuka, 'Resourcing Rangatiratanga as Part of Constitutional Transformation: Taking Equity and Sovereignty Seriously', *Kōtuitui: New Zealand Journal of Social Sciences Online*, 18, 4 (2023), pp.402–19.

8 Paul Tapsell, *Kāinga: People, Land, Belonging*, Bridget Williams Books, Wellington, 2021.

9 Ibid.

10 These consequences ranged from the unknown consequences of rāhui with teeth, to telling off, to death and war depending on the motivations and severity of the rāhui. See H.M. Mead, *Tikanga Māori: Living by Māori Values*, Huia, Wellington, 2003.

11 'Calls Grow for Rāhui to Have Greater Legal Recognition', 1News, 11 January 2022, https://www.1news.co.nz/2022/01/11/calls-grow-for-rahui-to-have-greater-legal-recognition/?fbclid=IwAR2s7PJ-FBBjTTiY2UuROlc_QYioRTk916zjtK9zPqcgUQnuaWAy79iuOuc (accessed 17 October 2023).

12 G. Harmsworth, S. Awatere and M. Robb, 'Indigenous Māori Values and Perspectives to Inform Freshwater Management in Aotearoa-New Zealand', *Ecology and Society*, 21, 4 (2016), pp.1–15; J.C. Kitson and H. Moller, 'Looking After Your Ground: Resource Management Practice by Rakiura Maori Titi Harvesters', *Papers and Proceedings of the Royal Society of Tasmania*, 142, 1 (2008), pp.161–76; J.P. Mika, K. Dell, J. Newth and C. Houkamau, 'Manahau: Toward an Indigenous Māori Theory of Value', *Philosophy of Management*, 21, 4 (2022), pp.1–23; M. Scobie, G. Finau and J. Hallenbeck, 'Land, Land Banks and Land Back: Accounting, Social Reproduction and Indigenous Resurgence', *Environment and Planning A: Economy and Space*, 19 November 2021.

13 M. Kawharu, 'Reinterpreting the Value Chain in an Indigenous Community Enterprise Context', *Journal of Enterprising Communities: People and Places in the Global Economy*, 13, 3, (2019), pp.242–62 as cited in Tapsell, *Kāinga: People, Land, Belonging*.

14 Tapsell, *Kāinga: People, Land, Belonging*.

15 Tapsell, 'Transitioning Environmental Governance in Aotearoa'.

16 We wrote this in a paper in 2020 but we're not sure that many people read it, so we're shouting it out again here. M. Scobie and A. Sturman, 'Economies of Mana and Mahi Beyond the Crisis', *New Zealand Journal of Employment Relations*, 45, 2 (2020), pp.77–88.

17 M. Stevens in L. Steyl, 'What Murihiku Learned from Past Transformations', Stuff, 10 January 2022, tps://www.stuff.co.nz/pou-tiaki/127258286/what-murihiku-learned-from-past-transformations? (accessed 17 October 2023).

18 Tapsell, *Kāinga: People, Land, Belonging*, p.55.

19 Though we don't want to let New Zealand's history as an exploitative imperial power in the Pacific off the hook either.

20 Capitalism is international, so alternatives against and beyond must also be international. We think it's important to look to the Pacific and build relations of international solidarity. See, for example: S. Vunibola, H. Steven and M. Scobie, 'Indigenous Enterprise on Customary Lands: Diverse Economies of Surplus', *Asia Pacific Viewpoint*, 63, 1 (2022), pp.40–52; S. Vunibola and M. Scobie, 'Islands of Indigenous Innovation: Reclaiming and Reconceptualising Innovation Within, Against and Beyond Colonial-capitalism', *Journal of the Royal Society of New Zealand*, 52 (2022), pp.1–14; Protect Pacific, https://www.protectpacific.com/ (accessed 17 October 2023).

21 And to be clear, people are starting to address this in scholarly work and on the ground. For example, Danielle Webb (Ngāpuhi)

wrote and researched an MA thesis on this topic: 'Marxism, Rangatiratanga and Māori Economies: Can the Rangatiratanga Sphere be Built Within Settler Capitalism?', MA thesis, Victoria University of Wellington, 2006, https://openaccess.wgtn.ac.nz/articles/thesis/Marxism_Rangatiratanga_and_M_ori_Economies_Can_the_rangatiratanga_sphere_be_built_within_settler_capitalism_/21824571

22 B. Jessop, *State Power: A Strategic Relational Approach*, Polity, Cambridge, 2007. Here Jessop interprets and builds on N.A. Poulantzas, *State, Power, Socialism*, Verso, London, 1978.

23 S. Barber, '"In Wakefield's Laboratory": Tangata Whenua Into Property/Labour in Te Waipounamu', *Journal of Sociology*, 56, 2 (2020), pp.229–46; M. Stevens, 'Te Ao Hou Realised or Te Ao Hou Redux?', panel discussion on Ngāi Tahu Settlement, Queenstown, 2016. For 'iwification' see Tapsell, *Kāinga: People, Land, Belonging*. And for more unfolding tensions, see J.P. Mika, G.H. Smith, A. Gillies and F. Wiremu, 'Unfolding Tensions Within Post-settlement Governance and Tribal Economies in Aotearoa New Zealand', *Journal of Enterprising Communities: People and Places in the Global Economy*, 13, 3 (2019), pp.296–318.

Acknowledgements

During the writing of this book, Evelyn joined us and Brian departed. We would like to dedicate the book to them.

We benefitted from the generous feedback of friends and mentors who took time to read through all or parts of this text with care. This includes Max Harris, Natalie Jones, Martin Fisher, Tyron Love, Phillippa Mein-Smith, Joshua Wilson Black, Rosalee Jenkin, Bill Lee, Stuart Rosewarne, Tayla Forward, Tom Baker, Andraya Heyes, Darian Woods, Antony Nihoniho, and Andre Poyser. All of your support, collegiality, friendship and time are so deeply valued.

Paul Schwalger at the Ngāi Tahu Research Centre also provided a lot of logistical and moral support over the time of research and writing. Everything you do is so appreciated.

We are also truly fortunate to have a large number of supporters and mentors that have not necessarily contributed directly to this text, but we are deeply grateful to nonetheless. You all know who you are.

Three readers gave us very useful and constructive feedback. Thank you to Morgan Godfery, Hautahi Kingi and Nancy Swarbrick.

Despite all of this feedback and support, we take full responsibility, and are accountable for the interpretations in this book.

Jane Parkin did the patient work of structural and copy editing with us. We are deeply grateful to Jane.

Thank you to everyone at BWB for supporting us through this process.

The researching and writing of this book was made possible by a Fast Start grant from the Marsden Fund, Royal Society of New Zealand Te Apārangi. This research and writing is part of a broader project on Indigenous Reconstruction: Rebuilding Indigenous economies from the ground up.

Finally, and most importantly we wish to acknowledge our loved ones for bearing with us on this: Megan Woodhouse and Evelyn Scobie, and Simon Hillier.

About the Authors

Matthew Scobie is Kāi Tahu (Kāti Huirapa) and Tauiwi. He grew up in Christchurch with limited exposure to Kāi Tahutanga but has been trying to slowly and humbly reconnect over the last decade. He teaches Indigenous economics and corporate responsibility in the Business School at the University of Canterbury. His research is committed to Indigenous reconstruction and draws from political economy and critical accounting.

Anna Sturman is a lecturer in Human Geography at the University of Sydney, on the unceded lands of the Gadigal peoples of the Eora Nation, where she works on the political economy and ecology of climate change. Anna was born and raised Pākehā in Te Waipounamu and much of her work brings together the two colonial-capitalist frameworks she knows best, Aotearoa New Zealand and Australia, in conversation with critical perspectives from across the world. She is committed to just futures for all.

About BWB Texts

BWB Texts are short books on big subjects for Aotearoa New Zealand. Over 100 Texts have been published since the series launched in 2013, available in print and digital formats. These can be purchased from all good bookstores and online from www.bwb.co.nz. To celebrate the milestone of publishing 100 Texts, starting from the 101st Text, each new title will feature its sequential number on the front cover.

BWB Texts include:

From Paper to Platform: How Tech Giants are Redefining News and Democracy
Merja Myllylahti

Why Memory Matters: 'Remembered histories' and the politics of the shared past
Rowan Light

Reconnecting Aotearoa: Loneliness and Connection in the Age of Social Distance
Edited by Kathy Errington and Holly Walker

Abolishing the Military: Arguments and Alternatives
Griffin Manawaroa Leonard, Joseph Llewellyn and Richard Jackson

Encounters Across Time
Judith Binney

Introducing The Women's Suffrage Petition
Edited by Jared Davidson, historical essay by Barbara Brookes

Introducing Te Tiriti o Waitangi
Edited by Jared Davidson, historical essay by Claudia Orange

Introducing He Whakaputanga: He Tohu Series
Edited by Jared Davidson, historical essay by Vincent O'Malley

Privilege in Perpetuity: Exploding a Pākehā Myth
Peter Meihana

The Best of E-Tangata, Volume Two
Tapu Misa and Gary Wilson (eds)

More Zeros and Ones: Digital Technology, Maintenance and Equity in Aotearoa New Zealand
Anna Pendergrast and Kelly Pendergrast (eds)

Pesticides and Health: How New Zealand Fails in Environmental Protection
Neil Pearce

Fragments from a Contested Past: Remembrance, Denial and New Zealand History
Joanna Kidman, Vincent O'Malley, Liana MacDonald, Tom Roa and Keziah Wallis

Kārearea
Māmari Stephens

Kāinga: People, Land, Belonging
Paul Tapsell

He Pou Hiringa: Grounding Science and Technology in Te Ao Māori
Maria Amoamo, Merata Kawharu and Katharina Ruckstuhl (eds)

The History of a Riot
Jared Davidson

100% Pure Future: New Zealand Tourism Renewed
Sarah Bennett (ed.)

Two Hundred and Fifty Ways to Start an Essay about Captain Cook
Alice Te Punga Somerville

First published in 2024 by Bridget Williams Books Ltd
PO Box 12474, Wellington 6144, New Zealand
www.bwb.co.nz, info@bwb.co.nz.

ISBN 9781991033741 (Paperback), ISBN 9781991033758 (EPUB), ISBN 9781991033765 (Kindle), ISBN 9781991033772 (PDF)
DOI https://doi.org/10.7810/9781991033741

A catalogue record for this book is available from the National Library of New Zealand. Kei te pātengi raraunga o Te Puna Mātauranga o Aotearoa te whakarārangi o tēnei pukapuka.

The publisher warmly acknowledges the significance of the ongoing support provided by the Bridget Williams Books Publishing Trust. The generous contribution from Ockham Residential for the BWB Texts series is gratefully acknowledged.

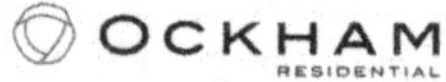

Publisher: Tom Rennie
Editor: Jane Parkin
Cover design: Neil Pardington Design
Internal design and typesetting: Katrina Duncan
Printer: Blue Star, Wellington